Skeps,
their History,
Making and Use

SKEPS,
THEIR HISTORY,
MAKING AND USE

by
FRANK ALSTON

Illustrated by
RICHARD ALSTON

NORTHERN BEE BOOKS
Mytholmroyd : Hebden Bridge

British Library Cataloguing in Publication Data

Alston, Frank
    Skeps: their history, making and use.
    1. Honeybee – Housing
    I. Title
    595.79'904564   SF532

ISBN 0-907908-38-1

Published by Northern Bee Books, Scout Bottom Farm, Mytholmroyd, Hebden Bridge, West Yorkshire © October 1987.

Printed by Lightning Source

CONTENTS

Picture Credits:

Cover and line drawings throughout: R. Alston.

Photographs–
M. J. Allan: Figs. 41 and 46.
R. Alston: Fig. 2.
E. Crane: Figs. 24 and 25.
B. Mobus: Figs. 42–45.
E. H. Pope: Fig. 31.
P. Sheppard: Fig. 48.
All other photographs: F. Alston.

PREFACE AND ACKNOWLEDGEMENTS

As beekeepers we tend to look forward. Each year brings its own frustrations but maybe next season will be all that's good, at least that's how it seems. Looking back, however, to the days of skep beekeeping enables us to appreciate the frustrations of our beekeeping ancestors, as well as the enjoyment.

Some fifteen years ago I began to be interested in bee boles, visiting known ones, and searching for fresh ones. The many miles travelled have brought their full reward, and I still keep searching for the many which I know have still to be discovered. They are our oldest beekeeping relics, and it is pleasing to record that although many have not withstood the ravages of time too well, there are also many which have been well cared for over the years and are still in excellent condition. I am extremely grateful to the owners and occupiers of properties who have received me so well and helpfully on my visits. They are far too numerous to mention by name. So, too, are the people who have helped me to locate fresh sites, but I am no less grateful to them also.

My interest in skep-making began at much the same time as my interest in bee boles, and the two interests, together with keeping the occasional colony in a skep hive, have helped me to a better understanding of skep beekeeping. To make a skep in the age-old manner, and with the time-honoured tools and materials, not only gives pleasure and satisfaction, but provides a tranquility not easily found in our modern world.

In addition to having received a great deal of assistance with bee boles, I have also been greatly helped by many people in various avenues of research into skep methods and equipment, and still others with valuable books of reference. All help, from whatever source, has been very willingly made available, and I thank these friends most sincerely.

Frank Alston.
Newlands, 33 Knowle Road,
Budleigh Salterton, Devon.

9

Swarms the bee the honey-maker

        H. W. Longfellow *'Hiawatha'*

Chapter 1

EARLY DAYS

Just when and how beekeeping began in Britain is not known, but it can readily be appreciated that in some very early times man tasted honeycomb from a forest colony of bees, and found it sweet to his taste. His discovery would encourage him to search for further colonies, and not to shun the task merely because bees had stings.

From this early honey hunting some method of primitive beekeeping eventually developed. As to how, we can only imagine that some honey hunter either carried back to his dwelling a hollow log containing a colony of bees, or perhaps a swarm from a hollow tree or rock crevice established itself at or near a dwelling, maybe in some upturned container or a sheltered cavity. What we can decide with certainty is that an elementary principle of beekeeping would soon be learned, that of ensuring a dry home for the bees, and we see this from the first known type of hive to be used in Britain.

This hive, sometimes referred to as an alveary, was made conical in shape, of willow or hazel woven around stakes and culminating in a point. Some method of filling in the gaps in the weave had to be evolved, and this was to daub the structure, both inside and outside, with a mixture we refer to as cloam or alternatively cloom. This cloaming, as the method is called, not only made the hive bee-proof but also weather-proof.

Various recipes have been given for cloam. Rev. Charles

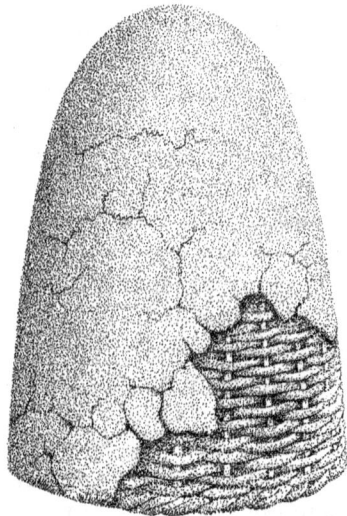

Fig. 1   A cloamed wicker hive

Butler in 1609 said "cow cloome tempered with gravelly dust, or sand, or ashes", and also said, in reference to hives "if they be not well covered are subject to wet which maketh them musty, and if it be much, rotteth the combs and destroyeth the bees". He also adds lime in a further reference to cloome in saying "keep the hives always close for the defence of the bees against their enemies. The best cloome for that purpose is Neats' dung: but to harden it, temper it with lime or ashes, with sand or gravel, which are also good against the gnawing of mice. With this cloome close up the skirts and brackes of your hives that there be no way into them."

Neats were working animals, oxen, as distinct from breeding cattle. Markham does not refer to the subtle difference in regard to the source of the basic material. His instruction was "make a stiff mortar of lime and cow dung mixed together, and then having cross-barred the hive within, daub the outside of the hive with the mortar at least 3 in thick down close unto the stone so that the least air may not come in."

A modern definition of cloam is earthenware, and it is interesting to note that the older Devon farmers often refer to field drainage tiles as cloam pipes. Also on Devon farms, floors in farm buildings were sometimes laid with a mixture of lime and clay which gave a very hardwearing surface. This material was similarly referred to as cloam.

In the area of Europe to the West of the River Elbe a straw hive was used, as early, says Dr Fraser, as the beginning of the Christian era. Its use spread further westward and was introduced to Britain by the Anglo Saxons. This straw hive we refer to as the skep, which continued to be used down the centuries until well into the present one.

The skep did not immediately replace the alveary, and in fact these wicker hives did not die out completely until into the 19th century. It may seem surprising that many beekeepers kept faith with the skep until relatively recently, but so it was, and it is known from records of the old Cumberland and Westmorland Beekeepers' Association that in 1906 almost 25% of all colonies of bees were housed in skep hives. It is of further interest that 25% of all colonies in these two counties, whether in wooden hive or skep were found, during the previous year, to have Foul Brood.

The name of skep is generally regarded to have been derived from the Norse word skeppa, meaning a container and measure for grain, equal to half a bushel. Some may feel that this is a strange definition in that a Winchester bushel of four pecks, varied for different types of grain. Thus in England a bushel was equal to 60 lbs of wheat, 50 lbs of barley, and 39 lbs of oats. Not only that, but there appears to have been appreciable variation in different localities. For example *The History and*

Topography of Westmorland and Cumberland compiled by Nicholson and Burn in 1776 says that a skep was an ancient measure equal to sixteen pecks Penrith measure, and that a Penrith peck was equal to two Winchester or Imperial pecks. It also says that corn was sold in Carlisle market by the Carlisle bushel, which was equal to three Winchester or Imperial bushels.

In order to get a clear picture of the meaning of bushel relative to skep capacity we must adhere to the Winchester bushel which is of 2150 cubic inches capacity, a half bushel being 1075 cubic inches.

To support this, Thomas Wildman in his *Treatise on the Management of Bees*, referred to a hive holding one peck which he said was 7 in deep and 10 in diameter, both measurements being internal. This size of hive has an approximate capacity of 550 cubic inches, which is one peck Winchester measure or thereabout.

Irrespective of the derivation it was not until into the 16th century that the name of skep began to be generally used in relation to bee-keeping. Prior to that time it was appropriately termed a hive.

From its introduction by the Anglo Saxons for use as a hive until the present time when its use is for swarm collection, various types of skep both in size and fashion have been used. Skep-making became a craft. Very often a beekeeper would learn to make his own skeps, but otherwise they were made by someone skilled at the craft, and trading as a skep-maker.

Today there are very few people skilled at the craft, although there has in fact been a revival of interest in it. Various methods are now used, but my own interest and fascination with it stem from the traditional materials, tools and methods of skep beekeeping days.

Whereas beekeeping methods changed very little down the years until the beekeeping revolution of 1851 brought about by Langstroth's invention of the movable comb hive, so the style of the skep hive changed very little and very slowly. Whatever change did take place did not alter the fact that beekeepers were still using a circular hive in which comb was attached at the top, and usually at the side.

Although straw was the general material used in skep-making, other reed was sometimes used in certain localities, particularly if straw was not easily available in that district. This local use often became traditional, and was not likely to change unless availability changed.

The traditional working tools of the skep-maker were simple, and cost virtually nothing. Their suitability for the job left nothing to be desired, and they are still used today. The age-old traditions of skep-making bring a fascination to the craft and add to the satisfaction which skill in it provides.

Chapter 2

SKEP-MAKING MATERIALS AND TOOLS

Proficiency and skill at skep-making by the craft of lip work comes gradually by practice. A first effort may appear to be irregular in shape and prove a little unkind to fingers in the making, but perseverance gives improved results and ultimate satisfaction at a job well done. The name lip work is derived from the Anglo-Saxon word leáp meaning a basket. It is now some fifteen years since I made my first skep, and I still get a lot of satisfaction from a job well done, not to mention the relaxation it affords in the making. One can readily appreciate the calm tempo of life of the old-time skep maker. He would never make a fortune skep-making but he was undoubtedly rich in other ways.

The materials used to make a skep with are some kind of durable reed, and a strong pliable binding cane. Several different kinds of reed have been used down the centuries and are still used today. In *The Nature Ordering and Preservation of Bees* written in 1614 Gervaise Markham said "To speak then of the Bee-hive you shall know there be divers opinions touching the same, according to the customs and natures of the Countries; for in the champian (flat open) Countries where there is little store of woods, they make their Hives of long Rye straw, the rowls being sewed together with bryers; and these hives are large and deep, and even proportioned like a sugar-loaf, and cross-barred within, with flat splints of wood, both above and under the midst part. In other champian Countries where they want Rye straw, they make them of Wheat straw, as in the West Countries, and these hives are of very large compass, but very low and flat which is naught, for a hive is better for his largeness and keepeth out the rain when it is sharpest."

He is in effect saying that straw is the reed to use, the type being whatever is grown in the locality and that the style of the hive should be tall and domed. In Britain wheat has usually been the more favoured and satisfactory cereal to be grown in the South of England, with rye, oats, and barley, being more commonly grown in Northern parts. Thus wheat straw has generally been used for skep-making in the South, and other straw, preferably rye, being used in the North. Rye, however, is no longer comonly grown. The bryers, referred to by Markham, are the brambles commonly found in many hedges and on wasteland throughout Britain. They provide an extremely pliable, firm and lasting binding, and have always been the authentic binding material used down the ages. The canes must be cut in late Autumn or early Winter when they are mature. These canes have to be stripped of thorns and side shoots, and ideally be stripped of bark. They are then to be split into about $^3/_{16}$ in strips, have the pith scraped from them and be allowed to dry.

Apart from rye or wheat straw, and to a lesser extent other cereal straws, there are other very satisfactory types of reed which have frequently been locally used. In parts of the South of England, Common Reed Grass, sometimes referred to as River Reed, growing profusely in some river estuaries, such as the Exe, was commonly used. Like wheat straw it made an ideal thatching reed, but for skep-making it needs to be cut during summer before it becomes too strong and brittle. Common rushes are believed to have been commonly used for thatching in the North of England, and were also used for skep-making there and in Scotland. They grow profusely in poorly drained land, but must be strong mature reed.

The *Victoria History of Lancashire* refers to the building of a house in the parish of Quernmore in the mid 15th century which was thatched with rushes, and although this does not confirm rushes to have been skep-making material, it is a fair indication of their probable use. I have made many skeps from common rushes, and although it is a very pleasant and easy material to work with it is not quite as durable as straw, in that the pith centre to the rush stems tends to make them a little more absorbent than straw. Also I have found it to be very necessary to bind a rush skep very tightly because warm summer temperatures tend to make the rushes shrink more than straw. Consequently there may be some slackness to the skep if not tightly bound. Moreover if used as a hive, slackness can result in the top of the skep becoming dished by the weight of comb and bees. Despite comparing rushes a little unfavourably with straw, I have used a rush hive regularly for fifteen years, and have found bees to work well in it. As yet the hive shows no sign of deterioration, and kept dry there is no doubt that it will still be in good condition in another fifteen years time.

A similar reed to the common rush is a species of sedge growing in the New Forest. It does not, however, have the same soft pith centre as the common rush, but is more straw-like. It is a strong and durable material, and in skep-hive days these sedges were cut to make a hive known as a New Forest Pot. The sedges were commonly referred to as bennets.

Fig. 2   Author making Purple Moor Grass skeps.

Another interesting material, still used in the North of Scotland where skeps are often called ruskies, is Purple Moor Grass. Dr. Crane in *Evidence of Welsh Beekeeping in the Past*, refers to skeps being still made from this material in Belgium. It grows in most parts of Britain in wet or damp peaty areas on moorland, such as Dartmoor, and in the fens. Alternative names are Flying Bent and Purple Melick Grass. The length of the stem is between two and three feet, but the stems are very slender. Having such a fine stem it would hardly seem to be a suitable material for skep-making. It does, however, make an extremely serviceable and long-lasting skep. When they were used as hives it is said that these skeps were more weather resistant than those of other reed. The explanation would seem to be that the finer stems bind more tightly and closer than thicker reed. I have used this reed on several ocasions for skep-making, and the result has been most attractive and very strong skeps, likely to keep their shape well over the years.

Purple Moor Grass is not an easy material to manipulate by reason of being extremely tensile. Hence it is necessary to use a coil narrower than when using straw, until a diameter to the work of about 8 in has been reached, and even then it is necessary to be still using a narrower coil than when using straw because of the spring-like tensile feature of the

16

Fig. 3   Purple Moor Grass skep.

the reed. A 15 in. diameter skep made with this reed weighs approximately 5 lbs while a straw one of the same diameter weighs about 3 lbs.

Just as straw is harvested in. Autumn so must other skep-making reed be cut at the same time, but if trial is being made of River Reed it must be cut a little earlier before the reed becomes fully mature and too brittle. It is necessary not to break skep-making reed, and it is for this reason that cutting by hand should be carried out, although straw cut without going through a combine harvester is quite satisfactory. After harvesting, the ears of corn are threshed or cut off. Straw dries quickly, but other reed, particularly common rushes, needs thorough drying. My own method with common rushes is to tie them in small bundles and hang them in a well ventilated shed or greenhouse. When tied green they dry to a pleasant golden colour in a few weeks. The tufted flowers must be removed before the rushes are used. Other reed must not only have heads removed but must be stripped clean of any attached leaves.

Whereas bramble cane was originally and traditionally used for binding, a more modern binding is basketry lapping cane. Equally as strong and durable as bramble, it is a much easier material to work with, and needs no special preparation. Moreover my experience has been that bramble can be a little brittle. In the Luneberg Heath hives were traditionally bound in the past with split spruce roots. This binding may have been used elsewhere, including Britain, but so far as I am aware no record or account of its use in these islands is known. The only other binding ever used seems to have been of hazel or withy thinly shaved, recorded by Gertrude Jekyll in *Old West Surrey*. They were said to have been used there and to have been described as lacings.

Skep-making tools are as simple and primitive as the materials. It is essential that the coils or ropes of reed, often referred to in the past as rolles, wreathes, or lissoms, shall be of an even thickness. To this end a gauge or girth is used into which the reeds are fed. The traditional gauge is a cow's horn with the end sawn off giving an internal diameter to the narrow end of the horn of about 1½ in. A cow's horn is not always easy

17

to acquire, but a metal ring or leather tube serve the purpose well enough as less authentic tools. An easily made one can be from a piece of hollow television aerial or similar piping of the right calibre. For stitching the cane into the reed, a so-called needle, traditionally being a hollow bone sharpened to a point is needed. The ideal bone for the purpose is a turkey-leg-bone "drumstick". Prior to the importation of the turkey into Britain during the 16th century a goose-leg-bone was commonly adapted. A similarly sharpened piece of metal tubing, or hard skewer-like piece of wood suitably grooved serves adequately as a needle, but neither has the same attraction in use as the bone needle. My own bone needle, after fifteen years of prodding its way through a hundred or more skeps, now has the polished appearance of ivory.

Although a beekeeper might often make his own skeps, skepmaking was a trade before the establishment of the movable-comb hive, and the simple tools which would last indefinitely were no doubt treasured and handed on to a son or other successor in the craft. Preparing bramble cane had its problems, and a simple tool for stripping was made by boring a hole well down the cavity of a cow's horn. The cane was then pulled to and fro through the hole and the open end of the horn, to remove the thorns and leaf appendages. It then became easy to clean the cane a little more, if desired, with a knife or other scraping tool. To split the bramble cane a wooden tool about six inches long and thick enough to grasp comfortably was used. One end of the tool had four flat sections, and the other end had three. The method of use was to push one end of the tool into the end of a length of bramble and continue forcing it down the full length. The thickness of the bramble dictated whether it should be split into three or four lengths.

Although in skeppist days a skep cost little to make, even nothing if a labourer could acquire a sheaf of straw from his employer or other friendly farmer, the rewards of labour must have been similarly meagre. In 1871 Geo. Neighbour & Sons advertised Common Straw Hives at 2s. 6d. each, which suggests that their skep-maker would be working for no more than 2 shillings per skep in providing them. At that time an agricultural worker's wage was about 10 shillings a week, and to him the purchase of a skep would be a heavy expense, no doubt meaning that, in many cases, the farm worker had to acquire the art and make his own.

At the present time a skep can still cost nothing if made from common rushes and bramble cane, but the cost of obtaining a nitche of straw from a friendly thatcher is very little and lapping cane can be bought at fairly modest cost. A nitche of straw would cost perhaps £3 and would make three skeps of adequate size.

18

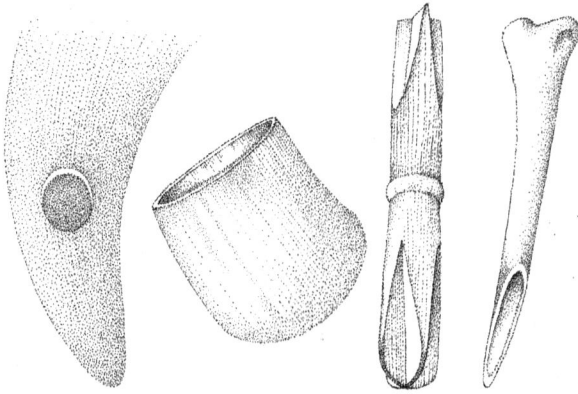

Fig. 4   Skep-making tools.

Cane for this number of skeps would cost about £5, although it does appear to be going up in price quite quickly. Even so it is still worth while for two or three beekeepers to get together and share the cost. Their first effort might leave something to be desired, but it would be far more reliable, I suggest, for the taking of a swarm than a cardboard box.

Chapter 3

SKEP-MAKING TECHNIQUE

In a dry condition both lapping cane and bramble cane are extremely brittle. It is thus essential to soak cane for several minutes before beginning to work with it. If bramble cane is to be used this must additionally be stropped, to make it adequately pliable, by placing one end of the length firmly under one foot, holding the other end in one hand, and then firmly rubbing down the full length with a strong piece of wood. The cane having been previously soaked, and having had the pith scraped from it, is now quite pliable and ready for use. It is quite unnecessary to strop lapping cane. What is a sensible precaution with lapping cane prior to use, is not to use too long a piece unless it is wasteful to do otherwise. About six feet is a convenient length. The reason for this is that the longer the piece the easier it is to twist it inadvertently, it takes longer to pull the length through when making a stitch, and the whole job takes longer to complete. Bramble makes its own length, which is not usually any more than 5 or 6 feet.

Reed should also be soaked for several minutes before use, at least until about half a dozen rounds of the skep have been built up, otherwise it tends to crack and not make such a smooth coil. It is essential to prepare reed before use by freeing it from any attached leaves, ears, or sheaths, and any flowers such as the tufts found on some common rushes. If this is not done a poor looking job will result, and certainly, if being used as a hive, numerous loose pieces prove an irritant to the occupants.

To begin the skep is the most difficult part. If a depriving hive, one with an aperture in the top, is to be made, the following procedure I find to be very satisfactory.

1. I take about twenty five soaked reeds and offset them slightly in length in relation to each other.
2. I then take a length of soaked cane and bind it very tightly round the reeds working from the butt end of them towards my right. *(see Fig. 5)* The binding should be started about 2 in from the butt ends, and the

Fig. 5   Starting a depriving hive.

Fig. 6   Stitching into the first binding.

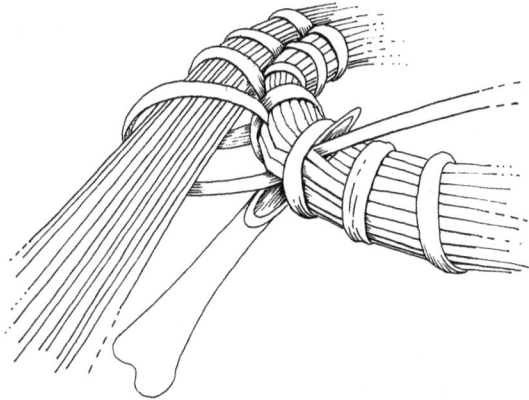

Fig. 7   Stitching under each successive binding.

Fig. 8   Ensuring a true circle.

otherwise loose end should be taken along the length of the reeds to be bound in with them as illustrated.

3. When some twenty bindings have been made I twist the rope into a circle, and keeping the cane tight I stitch into the first binding. The last two bindings must wrap into the circle the offset butt ends of the reeds. *(see Fig. 6)*.

4. Stitching now continues under each successive binding working from left to right. *(see Fig. 7)*.

5. To ensure that the circle is true and that it remains so, it is a good plan to push a short length of wood of the same diameter through the circle, or alternatively use a narrow jar. *(see Fig. 8)*.

6. The needle, when a stitch is made, must be consistently inserted parallel to the length of wood to succeed in producing the required flat top.

Stitching is very easy. The hollow pointed needle is pushed, slightly at a horizontal angle, through the reeds and under the next stitch of the preceeding coil until the point protrudes about ½ in. The cane is brought over the new coil of reeds and pushed through the groove of the needle and tightened. Before tightening this stitch, however, the previous one will have slackened, and must be re-tightened and held firm pending tightening of the latest one. *(see Fig. 7)*.

To begin a single or swarming hive, one without a top aperture, the following procedure is satisfactory.

1. Again take a bundle of about twenty five soaked reeds, but do not offset them as in the case of the depriving hive.

2. Taking a length of soaked cane bind the reeds as in the previous description, but starting some five inches from the butt ends of the reeds.

3. Put on only six bindings and holding them tight twist the bound reeds in an anti-clockwise direction into a tight knot as shown in *Fig. 9*, and make the first stitch into the first binding.

4. Continue to take the reeds anti-clockwise round the stitching under the remaining bindings of the knot.

5. To ensure that the knot is tight and firm it is necessary to pull strongly on both the butt ends of the reeds and just beyond the sixth binding, then holding the work firm as the first stitch is made.

6. Once the knot has been firmly made the butt ends of the reeds can be cut down almost to the level of the work.

Once either of the skeps described has reached the stitching stage the gauge is slid over the reeds, narrow end first. Additional reeds are inserted, butt end first, into the centre of the coil as stitching proceeds,

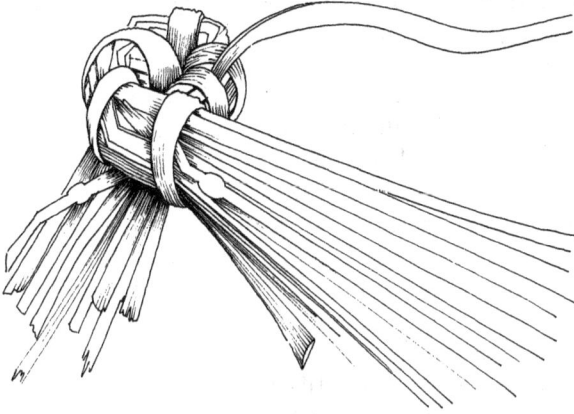

Fig. 9   Starting a single hive.

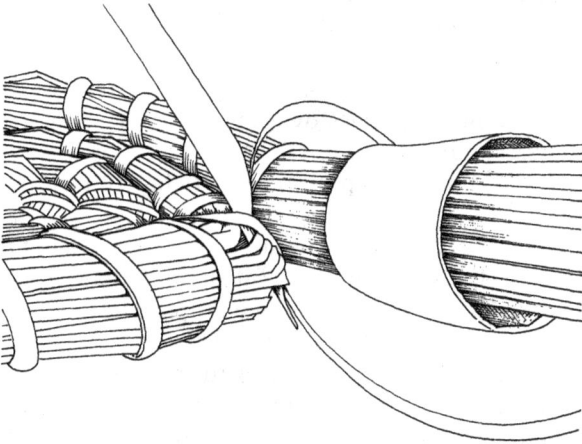

Fig. 10   Beginning a shoulder.

until its calibre gradually fills the gauge. Just as the thickness of the coil is gradually built up, the number of stitches must gradually increase by extra ones being made between stitches of the previous coil, until there are about thirty five in a complete round. When to make an extra stitch is suggested by available space between existing stitches of the previous coil.

If it is intended that the skep shall be flat-topped, then when making a stitch it is necessary to regularly insert the needle at right angles to the work. At a diameter of about 9 in. a start is made to build a shoulder to this flat top, prior to building the perpendicular sides. To this end insert the needle at an angle of about 60° to the work, as shown in *Fig. 10*, and continue to do so consistently at this angle until the internal diameter of the dish is 12 in., but this is variable according to the size of skep required. To effect the perpendicular side begin to insert the needle at right angles to the work again, making a start to do so at a point corresponding to where the 60° angle began, otherwise the skep may be a little out of shape.

When the skep reaches the necessary depth of about 9 in. the coil of reed should no longer be fed, and stitching is continued until the end of the reeds is reached. The end of the cane is then pushed through several adjoining stitches to give a firm and lasting finish.

Other features to be noted are how to join into the work a new length of cane, and how to secure the end of the preceding one. My method is to insert my new length of cane under the last stitch made by the previous length and pull it through to about 2 in. short of the end. This 2 in. I fold back to hook over the stitch it passes under. The first stitch of the new length can now be made to pass over and hold securely the end of the exhausted cane. The hooked end of the new cane is firmly held down under the coil and will not slip. I find this to be both a simple and efficient method.

As an alternative to giving a rounded shoulder to a flat topped skep this can be to make the side commence at an immediate right angle to the top. This is effected by inserting the needle parallel to the work so that the coil now passes beneath the last one.

A domed skep is shaped by inserting the needle at a varying angle in each coil to give a gradual curve, and in the latter stages to gradually bring the stitches to right angles with the work.

A relatively modern method of commencing a flat-topped skep is to cut a circle of about 4 in. diameter from 1 in. timber, and then to bore at about ⅜ in. within the circumference of it some thirty-five holes ³⁄₁₆ in. diameter. Into these the first stitches are made round the first coil of reed. An aperture can be cut in the block if desired. *(see Fig. 11)*.

In skep beekeeping an entrance to the skep hive was needed. The best means of providing this was for a 3 in. wide and ½ in. deep channel to be cut into the timber, or even stone, base upon which the hive was to stand. Alternatively the final coil of the skep needed an entrance built into it in the following manner. At the start of the final round make a

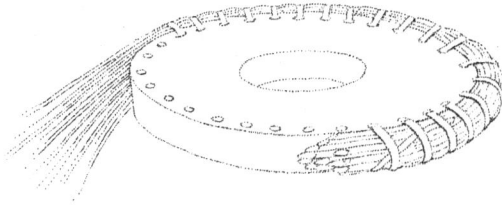

Fig. 11   Using a wooden ring on which to commence a flat topped skep.

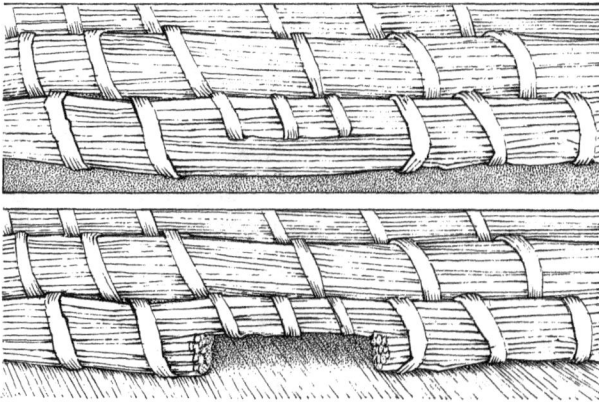

Fig. 12   Providing an entrance.

stitch through the middle of the final coil, and between the corresponding two stitches of the previous coil. Then stitch into the succeeding stitch of the previous coil and again through the middle of the final coil. Again stitch between the two corresponding stitches of the previous coil and through the middle of the final coil. Now continue with normal stitching, and cut out the unstitched portion of reeds. *(see Fig. 12)*

An old technique in skep hive making was to sometimes stitch onto a hoop of willow through which holes had been burned. The purpose of this was to avoid damage to the lowest part of it from mice, or by rotting from wetness of the hive base.

Chapter 4

COMMON HIVES

The skeps described in the previous chapter are collectively described as Common Hives, those without a top aperture being Single or Swarming Hives and those with an aperture, Depriving Hives.

Although from time to time one comes across well preserved skeps of probably a hundred years old, regrettably no skep has been preserved from beekeeping in ancient times. In 1950, however, the remains of one together with honey bees, was discovered at Coppergate in York and is believed to date from the 12th century. Nevertheless, it is evident from Rev. Charles Butler and Gervaise Markham writing in the early 17th century that single or swarming hives were then used, no reference being made to the use of depriving hives at that time. By the early 19th century we find the depriving hive being recommended by John Keys in *The Practical Beemaster.*

Fig. 13 Single hive in the shape favoured by Charles Butler.

The single hive was at no time made to any standard size. Charles Butler wrote, in his *Feminine Monarchie* in 1609 "The bees do best defend themselves from cold when they hang around together in the manner of a sphere or globe, and therefore the nearer the Hive comes to the fashion thereof the warmer and safer be the bees. But of necessitie the bottom must be broad for the upright and sure standing of the Hive, and for the better taking out of the combs." He goes on to give dimensions for a hive which "varies no more from this round figure than needs must". He envisaged a globe of 15 in. diameter, and a hive approximating to this size of 17 in. high and

26

and 13 in. wide at the mouth and 15 in. wide in the middle, having, he says, a capacity of three pecks. *(See Fig 13).*

In all common hives of any shape or size the insertion of spleets was necessary to prevent sinkage of the top of the hive by the weight of comb and bees, and the breakage of comb which can easily happen with soft virgin comb. Normally these were cross-sticks, each end being inserted in opposite walls of the hive. An alternative type of spleet described by Charles Butler for use with a domed hive incorporated what he called a cop. This was a round block of wood, at least 1 in. thick. On one side it was shaped into a dome, to fit inside the top of the hive. In the centre of the flat under-side of the cop a hole was bored for the spleets to rest in. To make the spleets a straight piece of hazel or willow was taken and quartered lengthwise. These four lengths were then fitted securely into the hole in the cop, cut down to suitable lengths, and the lower ends sharpened to points. The length was to be such that the sharpened ends pierced the sides of the hive at the third or fourth coil from the base or skirt of it. Some tension was given to the spleets by bending them slightly prior to insertion in the sides of the hive, with the effect that the points of the spleets holding securely in the hive sides enabled the tension given to them by the bending to push upwards on the cop, holding it firmly in position, and giving rigidity to themselves. *(See Fig 14).*

Fig. 14   Single hive of straw with bramble binding, together with Cop and Spleets.

Reverting to hive size, past writings confirm that, just as now, beekeepers have varying opinions on the most practicable hive size, so in skep days this feature gave rise to concern. It appears that the early skeps were usually smaller than those of later times. Swarming was acknowledged to be a natural trait of the honeybee, and early swarms were hoped for and encouraged by the tendency to use a small hive. Within this concept, however, there seems to have been no absolute concensus on the optimum size. Charles Butler said that hives should be of any size between a bushel and half a bushel. He said "The middling size of three pecks, or within a pottle under or over is most profitable".

A bushel skep (Winchester bushel pre 1826) had a capacity of 2150 cu ins, and one of three pecks, recommended by Charles Butler would, therefore, contain about 1610 cu ins. It is of interest to note that the capacity of a bushel skep approximated to the capacity of our present-day National hive, and from this it is a fair assumption that smaller hives would be conducive to the early swarm.

Some two hundred and fifty years later we find that Pettigrew, generally regarded as the master skeppist of his day, used skeps 18 in. and sometimes 20 in. wide and 12 in. high. These were internal measurements, giving a capacity of about 3050 cu ins, and even then he would frequently enlarge them with an eke. In the late 18th century John Keys recommended a hive size of 12 in. diameter and 9 in. high, giving only 1020 cu. ins. capacity. This seems to have been the general approximate size from the mid 17th century onwards until Pettigrew's time in the late 19th century, and it also seems that the flat topped hive had become favoured as distinct from the domed shape. This is probably due to the trend towards the depriving hive, and away from the single hive.

The depriving type of common hive provided for supering, or, to use the language of the time, "storefying". It was usual to use further skeps of the same size as the stock hive for this purpose, but alternatively a skep of smaller dimensions, usually refer-

Fig. 15   A depriving hive of common rushes knitted to a wooden ring in the crown.

red to as a cap, was used. The internal diameter of a cap would usually be about 9 in. and, being smaller than the stock hive, thinner coils of reed were used in the making.

Quite frequently these caps were made with a windowed aperture in the side of them, which enabled the beekeeper to observe progress within. The cap shown in the pho-

Fig. 16   A straw cap with window.

tograph has this aperture, and from information provided by the owner there seems to be no doubt that it is at least a hundred and fifty years old. It has been repaired to give it a new lease of life. The window seems likely to have been a disadvantage, in that although the beekeeper could, to some extent, satisfy his curiosity, it would not be easily fixed in position, and the necessary breaks in the coils of straw created weakness in the structure. This was also the likeliest part in which to find deterioration.

This idea of a window suggests frustration at the inability to judge the condition of a colony as we are able to do with a movable comb hive, since hives were likewise sometimes made with a windowed aperture.

In the second half of the last century Neighbour & Sons were selling such a hive with three windows in the side. In all respects it was much superior to the common hives, and had several refinements beyond the capability of skepmakers in general. The straw work was stitched to a wooden hoop to protect the skirt and to ensure firm standing. The top coil of the hive was stitched to a covering board containing apertures. Three framed windows covered by doors were fitted in the wall of the hive, with a thermometer positioned inside one of the windows. Clearly this was a hive for the relatively prosperous beekeeper. In the main, beekeepers used the common hive which, as Neighbour's catalogue said was "Of the simplest form, on the humane system, intended for use of the poor. Is recommended to the notice of the clergy and others interested in the welfare of the labouring classes". A salesman's comment was not necessary to point beekeepers towards the traditional common hive. In the main he had to economise to enjoy some profit, however meagre, and have pleasure from his bees. It is obvious, therefore, that the skepmaker's trade was essentially in making common hives.

Chapter 5

PROTECTION FOR HIVES

Our British weather was no respecter of the skep hive, and quite apart from cloaming, further protection against the elements was essential. Several methods were adopted, all aiming to keep the hive cool in summer, warm in winter, and dry at all times.

Hackle, or Coppet.

The use of a hackle was very common. As with the hive itself the material used in the making was long straw, rushes, or reeds tied to create a tent-shape to fit over the common hive like a hat, giving rise to the alternative name coppet. The simplest method of producing one was to take a sheaf of straw and tie it firmly round the neck. It was then opened out and placed over the hive. Round it was placed a gart which kept the straw' firmly in position round the hive. The gart was a hoop which not only kept the hackle firm but provided a means of securing the whole against wind in that ropes could be tied to it and be anchored to stakes in much the same manner as tent guy-ropes. The appearance of the heads of straw suggests the hackles or neck feathers of a cockerel when ruffled, which would seem to be how the name might have been derived.

Another method of making a hackle is described in a BIBBA leaflet on skep making. This is to loop together about twenty five reeds laid side by side, and then to tie to this a second looped bundle of the same number of reeds as shown in *Fig. 17*. Looping and tying of further bundles is continued until a width equivalent to the circumference of the hive for which it is needed is reached. This looping and tying is done some 6 in. above the butt ends. A second looping and tying is now done in the same manner mid-way down the length of the bundles, but in such a way that half of one bundle is tied to the adjoining half of the bundle alongside. The two looping rope ends are now tied together to form a tent shape, which when firmly tied around the head will fit snugly over the hive, and if a gart is provided the hive is well protected.

30

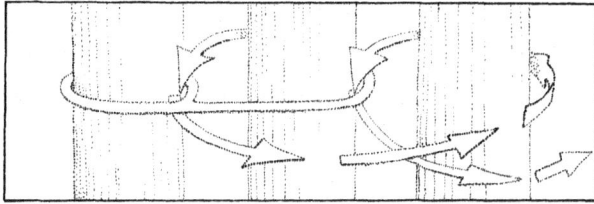

Fig. 17   Diagram illustrating hackle making.

I have personally made hackles from common rushes which have lasted three years before beginning to disintegrate from the effects of weather. In rain, rush hackles become sodden, as indeed do those made from straw, but in using them I have not found the hive underneath to become noticeably wet, beyond a slight dampness caused no doubt by the touching of the hackle at the shoulder of the hive.

The advice given by Charles Butler was "The hackle is now and then to be removed, not only to meet with mice, moths, spiders, earwigs etc which harbour under it, and to see what breaches the mouse and tit-mouse have made, but also to air the moist hive, and this in a warm and windy day after much wet".It is essential that the hackle should reach almost to the level of the hive base to prevent rain, particularly in windy conditions, soaking the sides of the hive and encouraging the skirts to rot due to water collecting on the hive base. *(See Fig. 18).*

Fig. 18   A hackle with a gart.

Pancheon or Creamer

Herrod Hempsall in *Beekeeping New and Old described with Pen and Camera* used the name pancheon. It is in fact a dialect word used in the North West of England as a name for an earthenware creamer, glazed inside and used for the settling of milk from which to obtain the cream. The usual capacity was six quarts. They were narrow at the base and tapered outwards to the top. If one of those utensils became cracked or chipped, and consequently no longer serviceable in the dairy, it was set aside by the good wife for use in the apiary. Inverted over a single hive the top and most of the sides of the hive were kept dry, although the lower part of the hive was not effectively protected from rain and snow. Some were of the opinion that they overheated the hive in summer. *(See Fig. 19).*

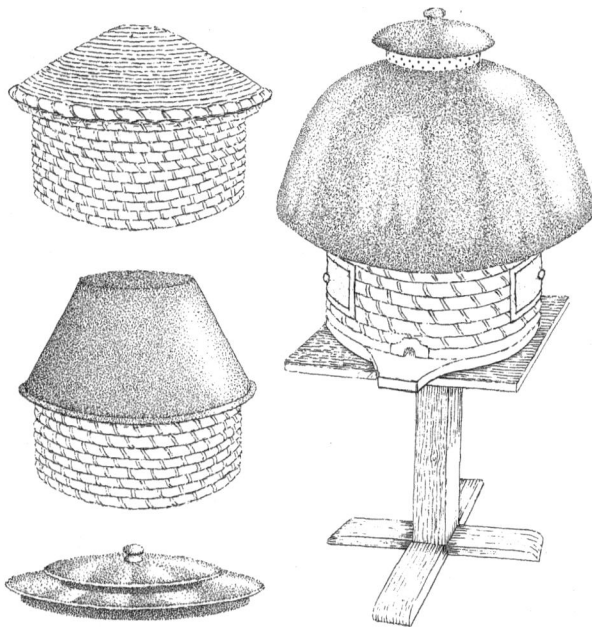

Fig. 19   Protection for hives.

Other covers.

Using the same principle as the inverted creamer, the appliance manufacturers, Neighbour & Sons, and no doubt others, were in the late 19th century, marketing zinc covers giving top protection to hives. Apart from limited protection their lightness must have been a distinct disadvantage in windy conditions. Skep-makers also produced a straw cover very much representing a Chinese coolie hat. It overhung the sides of the hive by some 3 in. and had a coil of straw stitched inside the rim to fit securely round the shoulder of the hive. Again it was light and afforded little protection to the lower part of the hive. *(See Fig. 19).*

Whereas hives themselves were frequently cloamed, an alternative was to make what can be described as a cloamed hackle. The method was to first stop up the hive entrance with earth, and then to thrust a quill through this to give ventilation. Straw was then placed over the hive in the same manner as a hackle was placed, but without any further fastening. Over the positioned straw, cloam was coated and left to dry. Once the cloaming had been completed the entrance was re-opened. Obviously the whole operation was carried out when no bees were flying, and conditions were dry so that the cloam would set. The whole cover was firm enough to retain its shape when removed, and was thus easily replaced. A hive cover made in this manner was said to last for two years.

A much less sophisticated method of giving hive protection was to place sods over and around the hive, with perhaps some material placed between the two. The skeppist certainly laid great store on keeping bees warm through the winter.

Chapter 6

SHELTERS AND BEE BOLES

To the cottager protection for the individual hive was essential. The more prosperous beekeeper, however, found some alternative protection to be advantageous, and to this end special shelters were constructed specifically to accommodate hives. There were many different types and styles, but they can be classified as either bee shelters or bee boles. Occasionally bee houses too were used which were sometimes for winter storage only.

Shelters

Free-standing shelters were often erected which were basically a stone or wooden bench over which was constructed a roof of wood, slate, or thatch. For still better protection they might be sited along a garden wall or house side, but if this was the case then the aspect must be approximately South. Charles Butler favoured having his hives facing a little to the West of South "to somewhat breake the East wind from the doore, and that the doore be lightened by the Sunne setting, when they return late and loaded from the field." Hives stood in such shelters may also have had individual protection as described in the preceeding chapter.

Other free-standing shelters were somewhat more permanent and distinctive. One style was suggestive of a series of adjoining dog kennels. Two good examples of this, which I have had the pleasure of inspecting, still exist in two Georgian residences at Lorton in Cumbria. They have slate rooves and brick ends, the rest of the structures being of wood. There are distinct compartments, each of which takes one hive. The bees could fly from front apertures, and behind are doors to provide access by the beekeeper. On the wooden floor of each compartment are two strips of wood, slightly more than bee-space deep, fixed at right-angles to the entrance in each case. Hives, unless they were very wide, would have to stand on these strips, and bees would have access at any point round the rim of the hive, and likewise come out of it. Whatever the real purpose of these strips may have been, my opinion is that they could have been intended to provide more ventilation than would otherwise have been the case. Additionally hives would not need to have an entrance cut in the skirt. *(See Fig. 20)*.

Fig. 20   An unusual shelter at Oak Hill, Lorton, Cumbria.

Fig. 21   Shelter at the College of Agriculture, Hartpury, Gloucester.

The College of Agriculture at Hartpury can proudly boast an outstandingly unusual structure, sometimes referred to as a bee house, but probably more correctly as a shelter, about thirty feet in length, with two tiers of recesses to take twenty four hives. It was previously situated at Nailsworth, but from there, at the instigation of the Gloucestershire Beekeepers' Association, and by the expertise of F. K. Potter it was transported to the College and re-erected there.

Apart from the impressive design and intricate workmanship the striking feature is that most of the stone in it is said to be Caen stone. The late E. G. Burtt established that in its original location at Nailsworth it was in the Manor of Minchinhampton granted by William the Conqueror to the Abbaye aux Dames at Caen where his daughter was Abbess. Dues from the Manor were said to be annually taken to Caen for delivery to the Abbess, and it is suggested that herein lies the connection from which stemmed the origin of the stone. This then seems to place strong emphasis on the fact that we can see here, not only a striking structure, but one of mediaeval date. Its preservation and re-erection reflects great credit to the County Association and the experts who made the task possible. *(See Fig. 21)*.

A further type of shelter was not free-standing but abutted onto the wall of either a garden, house, or other building. They were roofed with slate, or in the case of older ones they may have been thatched originally. It was often the case that in addition to the base shelf a second shelf above it was built to take a second row of hives. Very occasionally a third shelf was built, again to accommodate further hives. Existing shelters have sometimes retained the additional shelves, but often they have been removed to give very attractive garden shelters and seat.

One such shelter is still in existence at Nab Cottage looking out onto Rydal in the Lake District. Nab Cottage was built in 1700 and it is very likely that the shelter was built at the same time. De Quincey lodged at Nab Cottage for some time, and it subsequently became the residence of Hartley Coleridge. Wordsworth resided at nearby Dove Cottage, at which time Samuel Taylor Coleridge and Southey were residing in Keswick. Any of these distinguished persons may have sat in or near the shelter looking out over peaceful Rydal. *(See Fig. 22)*.

At Low Nest, a farm near Keswick, are the remains of a bee shelter. The present owner of Low Nest remembers her grandmother saying that bees were kept in the shelter in the late 19th century and that when her father died on 11th January 1897 the old custom of lifting the bees was performed. The superstition was that unless the hives were lifted and then replaced, the bees being told that their master had died and that

Fig. 22   Shelter at Nab Cottage, Rydal, Cumbria.

they were to accept a new master, they would either die or abscond. A similar custom in skep days was to tap on the side of the hive with a key and tell the bees of the death of the master, and it was not unusual for a piece of black material to be draped on the hive.

A very attractive shelter greatly adding to the charm of the garden, is at an isolated farmhouse, Moss Dyke in Mungrisdale between Penrith and Keswick in Cumbria. The house is dated 1730, and there is no reason to believe that the shelter is not of the same date. *(See Fig. 23).*

Mungrisdale is mainly an area of rough moorland and marginal land. Spring comes late there and bee flora is meagre, early pollen coming from whins and the very occasional willow or hazel. It seems miraculous that bees can survive there, let alone give a surplus, in such unfavourable terrain, and one is inclined to wonder why bees were ever kept there. There is, however, some scrubby heather which may well have been in better condition in an earlier age, but to me the answer lies in the faithful sycamore, in the dialect of the Cumbrians, and indeed of the Yorkshire dalesmen, "sackemer".

Fig. 23   Shelter at Mungrisdale, Cumbria.

At Moss Dyke and at very many Cumbrian hill farms, and also at those in the Yorkshire dales, at least one sycamore with its tassels hanging free in May can usually be found. I have seen colonies at a small apiary in Mungrisdale in late May with two completed National supers from this source. In passing I am prompted to say that in all my beekeeping experience in Cumbria and North Yorkshire I never knew the sycamore to fail to give a flow, and frequently a good one. In skep days in such areas sycamore, and in some instances heather, would be the main source of an appreciable flow, and to carry bees through the long winters it would certainly be vital to ensure colonies were well provisioned.

It is interesting to note that Herrod Hempsall in *Beekeepng New and Old described with Pen and Camera* draws attention to similar conditions on Luneberg Heath. He says "From the beginning of the Spring to the first of July bees in the Heath have not enough to live upon. You may ask, perhaps, how is it possible to keep bees in such a country?" For them the answer lay in migration at this lean time. Yes, thank goodness for the sycamore.

Sometimes owners of property where a bee shelter still exists have had the good sense to adapt it to use as a summer-house. A particularly

Fig. 24   Shelter at Tower Head, near Sawrey, Cumbria.

Fig. 25   Shelter at Crumlin, Gwent.

pleasing one is at Tower Head in Near Sawrey, a short distance from Beatrix Potter's home at Hill Top. The lower shelf serves as a seat, the others having been removed. *(See Fig 24)*.

The abutting feature of the shelters not only suggests buttress but also shooting butt to which they are very similar in appearance. It therefore seems natural to find in Dr Crane's *Archaeology of Beekeeping* that for a shelter near Ulverston in Cumbria the local name is given as butt. In Devon, however, I have heard the name butt being given on several occasions to describe skep hives.

As to the geographical distribution of bee shelters in Britain, Cumbria has the monopoly. At least thirty sites have been discovered in the county, but in many counties of England none have been found. In Scotland and Wales a few have been located, but none in Ireland. *(See Fig 25)*.

Bee Boles

The commonest form of shelter found in Britain is the bee bole, which is a recess within a wall and being part of it, as distinct from abutting onto it. The walls in which they are found are either those of a house or other building, or garden walls. Occasionally, as in the Yorkshire Dales, they are found in the wall of a field. One such example is at Wearing Fold near Giggleswick where bee boles are seen in a wall which joins onto a barn, or out-barn as described in that area, indicating it is not part of the main farmstead. It is quite possible, however, that a dwelling house may well have been there in time past.

Dr Crane regards the term bole as being derived from a Welsh word bolch, meaning a gap or aperture, and also quotes the *Scottish National Dictionary* as giving it to mean a recess in a wall. The word has been adopted for use as a beekeeping term in the rest of Britain. It is also interesting to reflect on the Danish word bolig, meaning a dwelling or habitation. Nowhere have I seen any comment to support my own idea that the word bole may have developed from bolig. Knowing that the skep was introduced to East Anglia from North West Europe by the Anglo-Saxons, however, it may well be , I feel, that bolig is the root from which the word bole originated.

What is known with certainty is that bee boles are, in the main, centuries old, although regrettably it is not usually possible to date them accurately. Occasionally the age of a house is known, but even this is not an infallible indication. I know one Devon bee bole site where it is known there was a dwelling in the 12th century, and although the present dwellinghouse does not date back so far it is likely to be 17th century at the latest. The bee boles there are in a stone wall which extends from a cob wall, and the boles themselves are inset into the stone but are built with standard brick, a relatively modern material. Here then is a case where the age of the house is by no means indicative of the age of the boles.

In 1953 Dr Crane and Mrs R. M. Duruz began a search for bee boles and other shelters in Britain. Since then other interested people have helped to locate sites, and the International Bee Research Association has, as a result, built up a register containing details and photographs of, at the present time, some thousand or so sites where there are bee boles or other bee shelters. New sites continue to be found, and it is certain that there are very many more still to be discovered.

The International Bee Research Association's record clearly indicates that the majority of known bee bole sites in England are in Cumbria, particularly in the Furness area of the county. Two other counties have a relatively large number of known sites viz. Yorkshire, particularly in the Dales, and Devon. These localities all experience heavy rainfall, and often very harsh winter conditions, particularly the Northern counties.

In the main, bee boles face between southerly and easterly directions, which means that they got some protection from our prevailing south westerly winds. This was a much more important consideration in skep beekeeping days than the fact that they got early benefit from the sun and enjoyed it for most of the day in summer, although the skeppists seemed to favour the sun theory. There are, however, a few exceptions to the general rule where, for example, boles have been built round a garden wall, or at the angle of two walls. This feature of added protection for hives was so vital that it is surprising we find little direct reference in past writings to bee boles, apart from the oblique reference to wall niches. In particular one would have expected Charles Butler to extol the virtues of the bee bole.

It is noticeable, however, that bee boles and bee shelters are most frequently found in residences of good standing, or properties which in earlier days had local importance. A property of modest standing would be less likely to be favoured with a garden or orchard of much size. Most beekeepers in recent skep days were cottagers, farm workers, and other country people of modest circumstances. It seems likely that the bee bole and other specially built shelters were for the more privileged, the less fortunate having to make do with a hackle or the old creamer only. The mere names of properties where bee boles are found are often indicative of a place of some standing. Many are farms, manors, halls, or rectories. In Devon the name Barton is sometimes incorporated in the name of a

Fig. 26   Well preserved boles at Landsend Barton, near Crediton, Devon.

Fig. 27   Single bole at Chilton, near Bickleigh, Devon.

property where bee boles have been discovered, for example Landsend
Barton, Star Barton, and The Barton. Barton is of Anglo-Saxon derivation, Beretun literally meaning "a corn farm", and referred to a detached
portion of a Manor or demesne farm.

In regard to the siting of bee boles at a particular property this may be in either the wall of the house itself, or the wall of an adjoining building, or quite often in garden walls. In Devon they are usually located in the cob walls of houses or adjoining cob-walled buildings, and in garden walls which are likewise very frequently of cob. Where built into cob the shape is almost invariably domed, with the arch springing sometimes from the base and sometimes from the sides. The back of the recess is either flat or alternatively rounded.

Many of these boles are still in excellent condition such as those at Landsend Barton *(See Fig. 26)*. Of cob, Professor Hoskins in his book *Devon* writes "It is impossible to say when cob was first used in the South West as a building material. In Devon, cob walling seems to have been known in the 13th century, and may even be older. Walls of cob houses vary in thickness. They are usually about 3 ft. and rarely less than 2 ft. 6 in. As a rule we may say the thicker the walls the older the building, and at times they can run to as much as 4 ft. 6 in. There is a view that cob originated in wattle and daub construction – perhaps a double wattle-work filled in between with mud." An old Devon saying is "all cob wants is a good hat and a good pair of shoes". Thus garden walls were thatched or slated, and built onto a foundation of stone. Houses were similarly built onto a stone foundation and were thatched.

An interesting cob wall where a single bee bole still survives is at Chilton near Bickleigh. *(See Fig. 27)*. In one wall of the house the owner recently removed cob to a depth of about a foot to reveal well preserved wattle and daub. Reliable opinion at that time was that the cob was 14th century, and if so this surviving bole is at least 600 years old. Again quoting Professor Hoskins from *One Man's England* he says "Devon is a mixture of more or less isolated single farmsteads or hamlets which are usually three or for farmsteads grouped together. Chilton is a perfect example of an isolated farmstead. It has always been isolated, never part of a bigger place. We know it belonged, as part of his Royal Estate, to Alfred the Great. In his will, made about AD880, he left his farm and a lot of other land to a younger son. Child's farm it means literally. So it belonged to Alfred in those days. I think it is even older than that." One is left with the very strong feeling from this fascinating knowledge that the Chilton bee bole may well be the oldest known one in Britain, although Professor Hoskins was not attempting to date the present dwellinghouse.

Another interesting Devon site is at Spencer Cottage in Coleford, once visited, it is said, by King Charles II. *(See Fig. 28)*. Whether there is any truth in this one doesn't know. Herrod Hempsall, however, makes

Fig. 28   Boles at Spencer Cottage, Coleford, Devon.

the interesting comment "King Charles II took such an interest in the hive-bee that he caused apiaries to be established at Whitehall in London, Windsor, and his park at Falkland in Scotland, all of which he used to visit frequently in order that he might see the bees at work." The bee boles at Spencer Cottage are situated directly under the eaves of an adjoining barn which would originally be thatched. Similarly high positions are seen at many other Devon sites. The overhanging thatch afforded protection from weather, and the height protection from ground predators. Also the flight path of the bees was kept well above passers-by.

Apart from being in cob walls we find some Devon boles to be in either dry stone or mortared stone walls. The naturally usual shape in stone walls is either square or rectangular, but sometimes we find the builder appearing to have been undecided in that they begin to be arched but are finished with a flat crown, as at Martin Farm near Whiddon Down. *(See Fig. 29)*.

A feature of the Northern scene is the dry-stone wall in which the majority of the Cumbrian and Yorkshire boles are found. A well built dry-stone wall can last for centuries, particularly at a homestead, where good repair is usually assured.

Fig. 29   Single bole at Whiddon Down, Devon.

The shape of Northern boles is usually square or rectangular, but domed ones do exist, two particularly attractive sets being illustrated *(Figs. 30 & 31)*. Both sets have taller boles than do their Devon counterparts, but the backs of them are similarly rounded. The Northumberland ones are unique in having a serpentine-fronted stone base, a most attractive feature. Brick is not a usual building material in Northern bee bole areas. Local stone is almost invariably used, a good example being at Long Marton, Cumbria, where the buildings are of red sandstone quarried nearby. *(See Fig. 32.)*

A favourite site of mine because it is so typically Lakeland is at a farm at the head of Thirlmere, where there is an adjoining sheepfold which in earlier times would be either an orchard or garden. Three boles are seen there, strongly and ruggedly built, seeming very much in character with Lakeland and its often harsh winter storms. They now

Fig. 30   Domed boles at Bank End, Hesket, Newmarket, Cumbria.

Fig. 31   Domed boles with serpentine fronted bases at West Farm,
Westerhope, Tyne and Wear.

have a use as stands for smitting bowls containing the smitting or mark-
ing fluid with which each sheep is given its owner's special smit or mark.
(See Fig. 33).

Fig. 32 Triangular arched bole at Town Head, Long Marton, Cumbria.

The manner in which the dry stone and mortared stone recess is fashioned is not standard. Sometimes boles are several feet apart or they may be adjoining, separated only by piers. Usually they are in a single row, but a two or even three tier arrangement is sometimes found. Sometimes the base extends a few inches beyond the face of the wall, and sometimes there is an overhang above to shed the rain. The backs of the recesses are invariably flat. This fashion of building is not restricted to Northern counties.

In some parts of Britain brick is a common building material, and in the South East we frequently find bee boles built into brick walls, and we find them to be generally gabled or domed. A

Fig. 33 Boles at Bridge End, Thirlmere, Cumbria.

common feature of these brick recesses is that they do not extend as deep into the wall as do others. Often they are no deeper than 12 in. or even less. Frequently the height and width are also less than elsewhere, to such extent that it sometimes becomes questionable whether a hive could be accommodated. Certainly they could not take a storefied hive.

Nowhere in Britain is there any standardisation of size, but where boles are mainly to be found, viz. Cumbria, Yorkshire, and Devon, we do find that those of Northern Counties are larger than those of the South West, which in turn are larger than those of the South East. Again the query comes to mind as to what this indicates in regard to hive size and beekeeping practices in the relative regions. The height of the South West domed boles makes them capable of taking a tall domed hive, whereas the Northern ones are very much wider and higher, which not only suggests a tall hive but also a storefied one. However, the age of many of the Northern ones pre-dates the introduction of storefying, so that this comparison of size tells us nothing in regard to hive size and practice in the various regions.

As we know nothing from skep day writers about bee boles, we can only guess that perhaps the larger Northern sizes were to enable straw or other insulation to be packed round the hives in the winter months, since warmth in winter seems, for many skep day writers, to have been essential for survival and colony prosperity. This belief in packing seems to have outweighed the greater need of colony strength to combat the cold of winter.

Bee boles and bee shelters are Britain's oldest beekeeping relics. To some they may be of no more than passing interest, but each has its own individuality, and finding fresh ones or visiting known sites for the first time has a thrilling fascination. The only disappointment comes from not being able, in many instances, to ascertain the age of the bole or shelter.

In addition to those already mentioned a few more bole and shelter sites are worth special mention. Most of us are familiar with Beatrix Potter's children's books, and in Jemima Puddleduck Beatrix has an illustration of bee boles. These were at her home, Hill Top at Near Sawrey in the Lake District. They are faithfully depicted, even to the rhubarb patch in front of them, which, like the boles, is still there. Although she gives a false impression of their use by wrongly showing a wooden hive standing in one, this does in fact clearly indicate the relatively large size which is a feature of most Cumbrian boles. In height at least, they would, in many instances, have accommodated a supered wooden hive. That particular bole would take two storefied straw hives. *(See Fig. 34)*

Fig. 34 Boles at Hill Top, Near Sawrey, Cumbria.

Fig. 35 Shelter and boles adjoining Dove Cottage, Grasmere, Cumbria.

In the garden adjoining Dove Cottage in Grasmere, the home of William and Dorothy Wordsworth, are bee boles and a bee shelter. Dorothy, in her Grasmere Journals of 27th January and 27th April 1802 refers to bees being kept at Dove Cottage on a bee stand. Her April reference said "John Fisher had sodded about the bee stand." The shelter has obviously been re-roofed in recent years with the appropriate Lakeland slate, to good effect. There are ridge slates to the roof which have been uniquely fixed into position with slate pegs, the technique being known in Lakeland as 'wrestler's grip'. The name is said locally to be derived from the Cumberland and Westmorland style of wrestling grip which is that the fingers of each wrestler interlock into the palms of the hand behind the opponent's back thus firmly fixing the arms in an almost unbreakable grip. Long may the ridge slates at Dove Cottage remain unbroken. *(See Fig. 35)*.

Bridge Field Farm at Spark Bridge near Ulverston in Cumbria, believed at one time to have been in possession of the monks of Furness Abbey, has a set of five bee boles built in a dry stone wall on a hillside in step fashion. *(See Fig. 36)*. This is an unusual feature, but necessitated by the rising ground, of course. Another site where this is seen is at Newton Ferrers near Plymouth, again because of the rising ground.

Fig. 36   Boles in step fashion at Spark Bridge, Cumbria.

51

Blands Farm near Wennington on the Lancashire and Yorkshire boundary has an intriguing sunken garden with, at one time, eleven boles though only seven now remain. *(See Fig. 37)*. They are set into the wall surrounding the garden, more appropriately known as a bee garth. The age of the present house is 1690, but the whole property site has Roman, Anglo Saxon and Mediaeval features. The garth is but a few yards from the dwellinghouse, a barn, and an ice house. From this property a tunnel runs to Robert Hall, a venerable building about a mile away, which in Catholic times had a domestic chapel attached. Also about a mile away ran the Roman road from Ribchester to Tebay, and pillars under the present house are said to date from Roman times. The bee boles could certainly date back to mediaeval times, but regrettably this cannot be firmly established. The translation of a writing by Palladius, and quoted by Dr Fraser fits this setting admirably.

> "The bee-yerd be not ferre, but faire asyde
> Gladsum, secrete, and hoote, alle from the wynde.
> Square, and so big into hit that no thef stride.
> Thaire floures in coloures or her kynde
> In bushes, treen, and herbes thai may finde;
> Herbe origane, and tyme and violette,
> Eke affidille and savery therby sette."

Fig. 37 Blands Farm, Wennington, Lancashire, showing bee garth and ice house.

The ice house not only promotes the idea of age to the site, but brings to mind Dr Crane's quote in *Archaeology of Beekeeping* taken from the Agricultural Survey of Aberdeenshire of 1811. "The great objection to the keeping of bees is the expense of feeding them in an unfavourable spring. An ingenious friend of the reporter's has contrived to keep them in an ice house in a state of insensibility, which is a saving of their winter provisions." The idea seems somewhat extreme, and very much in contradiction of the generally accepted skeppists' principle that bees should be kept warm in the winter months. Certainly they would be kept dry, and strong healthy colonies with adequate stores would take no harm.

Where individual boles adjoin each other, the only division between them is a narrow pier, as is the case at many Northern sites. Sometimes the pier is a single roughly hewn slab of some 6 in width, though occasionally it may be dressed stone, and at Burton Hall at Burton Leonard in Yorkshire is a fine example of Tudor brick piers. The particular wall into which this set is built is in fact subject to a preservation order. Many owners feel pleased to have such old and unusual features as part of their property, and try to maintain bee boles and shelters in good condition despite the absence of preservation orders, which are not usually imposed. *(See Fig 38)*

Fig. 38 Well preserved boles with Tudor brick piers at Burton Hall, Burton Leonard, Yorkshire.

Gloucestershire has very few known sites, but apart from the exceptionally impressive shelter at Hartpury, there is an unusual case at Bourton-on-the-Hill where at the Manor House in a Cotswold stone boundary wall of the garden there are three boles with a further single bole in the same wall but on the other side of it, and, of course, facing in the opposite direction to the three. So far as I am aware this is the only case in Britain where boles are on the opposite side of the same wall.

Two sites which could well be the oldest known ones are found in Devon. At Buckfast Abbey *(See Fig. 39)* are three boles in an old stone wall. These are thought to possibly date back to the 12th century. The original Abbey was founded in 1018, but the buildings fell into disrepair after dissolution in 1539. Bro Adam confirms that there were four boles until recently, but how many there may have been originally is not known.

Fig. 39   Boles at Buckfast Abbey.

Another set at The Ring o' Bells in Cheriton Fitzpaine *(See Fig. 40)* is probably 14th century, and is still in very good condition in the cob wall of the inn. A recently erected additional building has covered two of the original boles but two still remain, one of which is rectangular and has a door at the back. Prior to being an inn the site comprised a row of cottages occupied by monks during construction of a nearby church in the mid 13th century. It seems, from mention in the Domesday Book, that an Inn existed which probably adjoined the monks' cottages and subsequently

Fig. 40   Boles at the Ring o' bells, Cheriton Fitzpaine, Devon.

was extended in place of them. Part of the floor of the inn presently there, which stands on a slight slope, has several levels corresponding to the floors of the previous cottages.

Scottish bee boles seem on the whole to be generally a little larger than those in the North of England, and certainly are much larger in the main than those in the South. Like Northern England's bee boles, and many in Cornwall, the shapes in Scotland are usually rectangular,

Fig. 41   Rebated boles to accommodate doors at Edenshead, Gateside, near Cupar.

Fig. 42   Boles at Lieurary Mains
Near John o'Groats.

Fig. 43   Arched bole with jambs of
tooled stone at Pluscarden Abbey,
Elgin.

whereas those in Devon are usually arched or domed and those in Kent usually being with gabled or triangular tops and distinctly smaller in size.

Very occasionally English bee boles are found to be rebated to accommodate doors, but in Scotland this is a much more common feature. At Gateside near Cupar in Fife is a set of six with a rebate and old hinges still visible to accommodate doors. The photograph clearly shows the rebate. *(See Fig. 41)*.

Several other photographs are shown of interesting Scottish bee bole sites. At Lieurary Mains near Thurso in the Highland Region *(See Fig. 42)* is a set of four gabled boles and one of these is shown. This gabled shape is certainly not common in Scotland. Although in stone and not red brick like many in the South East, and Kent in particular, it is of the same shape. This site is almost at John o'Groats and only two other sites, which are known, can lay claim to being a mere five or ten miles nearer to that landmark.

Pluscarden Abbey at Elgin *(See Figs. 43 and 44)* has two separate sets of two boles in each. One set is built with jambs and arches of tooled stone. The other set is also distinctive in that the rough stone has been skilfully fashioned to the same domed shape as Devon cob boles. The Abbey is said to date from 13th century, but whether the boundary wall in which the boles are sited is of the same age is not known. At Midmar Castle near Inverurie *(See Fig. 45)* are two gabled

Fig. 44 Domed bole in stone wall
at Pluscarden Abbey, Elgin.

sites hardly any are in the West but are located mainly in the East, with very many of them being near the coast, and the main concentrations being in Tayside, Fife, and Lothian. One wonders why this area, Cumbria, West Yorkshire, Devon, and to a lesser extent Cornwall and Kent should have more bee boles and shelters than other parts of Britain. In all these areas of concentration there has been relatively little development through the years. The Yorkshire Dales and much of Cumbria are clear

structures about six feet high which project about 14 in. from the wall into which they are built. Here also the surrounding edges are rebated to take doors. The present louvred ones are a recent addition. The gabled top carries a pediment and the whole has a most attractive appearance. A further example of structures which project from the wall is near Cleish in Tayside. It is interesting to note that whereas sandstone is used for the slabs of the structure, the wall itself is of brick. *(See Fig. 46)*.

The records of the International Bee Research Association show that of the known Scottish

Fig. 45 Alcove at Midmar Castle, Inverurie, with doors and pediment.

57

Fig. 46   Projecting sandstone boles in a brick wall, at Annacroich House near Cleish.

examples of this. Agriculture there has escaped the enlargement of units and the modernisation of buildings to any marked degree. Villages and hamlets have frequently not been molested so that bee boles there may often have survived to today.

The Furness area of Cumbria, once part of North Lancashire, has a very high concentration of bee boles and bee shelters, but the remainder of Lan

Fig. 47   Winter storage accommodation in St. Dominic, Cornwall.

cashire, where farming is more intensive and where there has been more industrial development, has relatively few known sites.

In Devon many villages are very small, often comprising only a mere handful of houses. Devon sites are frequently in cob walls. In the main the existing cob houses were built in the 16th and 17th centuries, and it is interesting to note that whereas cob was the traditional material in East and North Devon it is in the belt running from Exeter in the East to Barnstaple in the North that most bee boles have been discovered, usually in the well preserved cob houses or cob walls of these charming Devon villages showing little change.

A few sites are known where a building provided storage for hives during the winter months. Such buildings had recesses inside one or more of their walls in which the hives were placed. They were dark, and provided a fairly constant temperature so that bees did not fly and food consumption was low. The hives were taken outdoors early in the year when the weather became favourable. It would seem to have been sensible to make outlets through the back of the recess to permit bees to fly out, thus avoiding the need to take colonies outdoors. It was not customary to make such outlets, but a site is known at St. Dominic in

Fig. 48   Boles in three tiers at Blackhall Farm, Castle-upon-Alun, Glamorgan.

Cornwall where they were provided. *(See Fig. 47)*. Regrettably the building is falling into disrepair but the present owners hope to restore it. In an end wall are twelve recesses. It is possible that this winter bee house and others like it may have had some additional use. It is small, measuring internally about 10 ft. by 12 ft., but even that is larger than a winter bee house in Devon, which measures 10 ft. by 7 ft.

Wales has relatively few known bee bole sites as compared with the rest of Britain. They are concentrated in South Wales, particularly Glamorgan. At Blackhall Farm, Castle-upon-Alun, is an unusual set of boles built in three tiers which has been kept in excellent condition. *(Fig. 48)*. Ireland and the Isle of Man have still fewer known sites. Those in the Isle of Man are found in the East of the Island, but there is no particular concentration in Ireland.

Chapter 7

HIVES AND BEEKEEPING PRACTICES

Of practical beekeeping in Britain up to the 16th century we know little. It might be thought that the Romans would introduce their hives and methods to Britain, but we have no evidence that this was the case, and it appears that the wicker hive was the only kind to be used until the Anglo Saxons, who invaded Britain in the mid 5th century, introduced the straw skep as an alternative hive. The skep did not totally replace the wicker hive, and both were used, but with the skep gradually proving to be the more popular.

Honey was obtained from hive bees as well as being collected from wild bees in the forests. Indeed in 1225 by the Charter of the Forests the taking of bees, honey, or wax, from the propery of the owner was poaching, in that the wild bees were as much the property of the owner as game. Under this Charter a case was brought in 1229, honey having been taken from the Royal forests of Quernmore and Wyresdale in North Lancashire and taken to the nearby home of one Ralph de Caton. The poachers, it seems, burned the tree from which the honey and byke of bees were taken. The value of the tree was 4d and that of the honey 6d. A freeman, however, was perfectly entitled by the Charter to collect bees and honey from his own forest or woodland.

The Anglo Saxon period in Britain was characterised by the Feudal system. The whole Anglo Saxon community was frequently spoken of as consisting of Eorls and Ceorls who were respectively nobles and common freemen. The Former were men of property and position, and the latter were smallholders, handicrafts men, and others with a skill, who generally placed themselves under the protection of a noble who thereafter was termed their Lord. Besides these there was a class of serfs who were either born as such, or had forfeited their liberty, perhaps by crime or poverty. These served as agricultural labourers to their masters' estates, and were as much the property of their master as his animals and chattels.

Of the freemen the beekeeper, or beo-ceorl as he was known, and the swineherd, were the lowest ranking. The beo-ceorl held his bees and his land from his Lord. He probably had to care for the bees of the whole Manor, and in some instances his land may have been granted to him in consideration of so doing. On the death of the beo-ceorl the land he had been granted, and his bees, reverted to his Lord. If the beo-ceorl had a son it was usual for the Lord to invest the son with any land and bees which his deceased father had held. In Norman times the beo-ceorl became known as custos apium.

Apart from limited knowledge of hives, we know little of beekeeping practice up to the end of the Middle Ages. The skep hive was almost certainly conical, in line with the style of the wicker hive, and in many instances was cloamed likewise. Markham, in the early 17th century, described both wicker hives and straw hives as being "like a sugar loaf", and Rev Charles Butler in 1609, describing the straw hive, speaks of "the concavity of the top of it." They were not including a flat-topped skep or straw hive, and there would seem to be no doubt that conical was the shape both then and earlier. These straw hives were, of course, single hives with which the storefying system could not be adopted.

Although sugar was not imported in the Middle Ages the use of honey as a sweetener or a food was often secondary to its use in making mead. Wax was in high demand by the church for candles until the 1530s when for a few years there was a temporary decline in demand and for the same purpose in the homes of the nobility, not only for light but also for time keeping.

> When life on earth had just begun,
> Man's only clock was the golden sun,
> But wise King Alfred found a way
> For telling of the time of day.
> He called a candle to his aid,
> And for every hour a notch was made.
>
> (Hugh Chesterton)

The less prosperous made do with rush lights, which were reeds dipped in beeswax, but the poor had to resort to tallow candles made from mutton fat.

Another less common use of wax was in burial. Nobility were sometimes buried in waxed shrouds, cere cloth. An intriguing discovery was made at St Bees in Cumbria in 1984. The scene is at the church there, which between 1130 and 1539 was part of a small Benedictine Priory housing a prior and six monks.

Recent excavations revealed a lead-wrapped body. A paleopathologist examined the body, believed to pre-date 1539 and to have probably been 14th century. Inside the lead covering, two linen shrouds were wrapped round the remains, and were impregnated with a tarry sticky substance. The shrouds proved to be amazingly intact and analysis of the coating suggested beeswax. One wonders why sufficient tests were not carried out to prove the suggestion of beeswax.

The report also said that the body, that of a man, had a recognisable Mediaeval face. The whole body, although darkened with age, was remarkably well preserved, showing some hair, a moustache, teeth, hands with nails and palm lines. In view of the report saying that the shrouds were impregnated with a tarry sticky substance it would seem that the beeswax contained additives.

According to Charles Butler there were several recipes for preparing a cere cloth. He was in fact describing a kind of poultice for wounds or body ailments when he said "A cere cloth or ceratum, so called of cera, doth consist chiefly of wax and oile mixed in such proportion as may make the ointment of just consistence, and therefore being made in summer or compounded with turpentine, lard, gum, marrow, or any liquid thing, a greater quantity of wax is required, and being made in winter or compounded with rozin, pitch, metals, dried herbs, powders or any dry thing a less quantity of wax than oile is convenient." Although he makes no reference to burial it does seem likely that wax used for a burial cere-cloth would have additives to enable the linen to absorb much of the emulsion, and his recipes certainly suggest the tarry sticky substance with which the St Bees shrouds were impregnated.

From Rev. Charles Butler's Feminine Monarchie written in 1609 we really come to learn about skeps and skep usage. A scholar, with a sound knowledge for his time of bees and beekeepng, he gives a clear picture of practical beekeeping, based on his own experience, and much of what he says is as true now as it was then. Moreover his style makes the reading of his work a real joy. At that time the single or swarming hive was the style used. The use of a depriving hive, which could be supered, or storefied as the method was called, may have been introduced by Charles Butler, at least he was the first person to have been known to describe it, but in practice he used a single hive. He preferred his 3 peck size to the much smaller 2 peck size which was generally favoured by beekeepers at that time.

The aim and hope in using the single or swarming hive was, as the name suggests, to obtain swarms from the colonies housed in them, and obviously early ones. Not only was it important that a swarm had time to build up well, and hopefully be well furnished with stores in the autumn, but also that the parent colony should be able to produce a new queen and have time to also build up and furnish itself well before the end of the season.

It was also essential that a beekeper should increase the number of his colonies through swarming, to counteract winter losses, and to enable him to forfeit some of his colonies in the autumn if he were to take any honeycomb from them. At that time he selected the heaviest and lightest of his hives from which to take the honeycomb, leaving those of medium weight to, hopefully, survive the winter.

There were two accepted methods of taking the honeycomb. One method meant completely sacrificing the bees of a selected hive by suffocating them. To do this circular pits, slightly less in diameter than the hives, were dug and in them split-ended sticks holding paper which had been dipped in brimstone were planted. They were then lit and the hives were placed over the pits. Sealed around the skirts with earth the hives were left several minutes to allow the fumes to circulate. The hives were then removed and shaken to rid them of any lingering bees which had not fallen into the pits.

The murderous deed completed, the hives were removed from the apiary and the comb containing stores and quite frequently some brood also was cut out, the whole being then squeezed in a honey-poke to get the honey, and wax from the residue. Not an easy task for a kindly beekeeper who must have had to steel himself for the ordeal.

A slight variation from the use of the brimstone papers was to light a small fire in the pit and then scatter flowers of sulphur on the glowing embers as the fire subsided. No matter how much care was taken in sulphuring, contamination of the honey could easily arise. An instance arose in 1457 where a case was brought against a Richard Ruddyng for selling honey said to have been adulterated with sulphur.

It was sometimes the practice in sulphuring bees to somehow place either a cabbage leaf or rhubarb leaf above the burning strips to avoid falling bees extinguishing them.

The illustration *(Fig. 49)* shows a shielded container which had been left lying in a bee shelter at Lorton in Cumbria. With the container was a canister filled with flowers of sulphur. Inside the shielded container was a shallow dish capable of holding inflammable material upon which the sulphur could be scattered. No reference appears ever to have been made to the use of this kind of equipment for sulphuring, but it certainly seems very probable that it was used for this purpose at the location where it was discovered.

The alternative to sulphuring was to drive the bees from the hive being taken up, a method very much favoured by Pettigrew in the mid

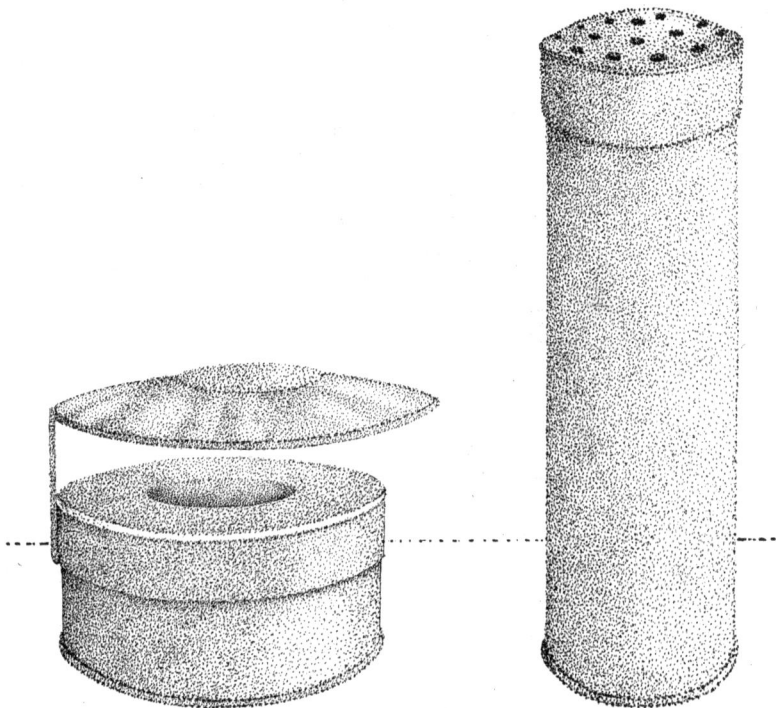

Fig. 49 Shielded container and canister.

19th century. Driving entailed inverting the lifted hive, standing it in some kind of container such as a bucket, and skewering to the mouth at one side, the mouth of an empty skep, the skewering being done in such a manner that the direction of the comb was towards the point of attachment. The skep was secured at an angle with driving irons, fixed in the walls of both hive and skep. It was usual to cover the space between the two with a cloth. The sides of the hives were then firmly drummed, thus causing the bees to run into the empty skep as illustrated in *Fig. 50*. The beekeeper could then either cut out part of the comb and return the hive to its site, shaking the bees from the skep in front of it to run back, or he could cut out all the comb.

In the latter case, however, the bees would not survive the winter if the driving was done in the autumn. Pettigrew, if he cut out all the comb

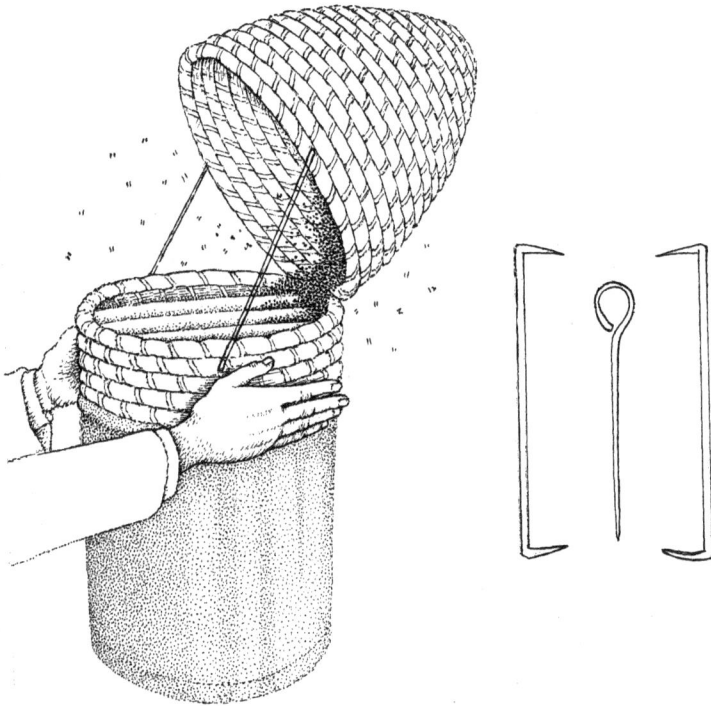

Fig. 50   Driving bees.

would unite the driven bees to a colony, preferably in the evening, by giving a good sprinkling of thin syrup strongly scented with mint to both the stock and driven bees, and then shaking the driven bees over the mouth of the upturned hive containing the stock.

To obtain honeycomb from a single hive was neither easy nor anything other than distressing in the case of sulphuring, and by the early part of the 18th century, use was being made of the depriving type of common hive, enabling a crop to be harvested without destruction of bees.

The principle was that in the top of the hive was an aperture of about 3 in. diameter, permitting the bees to ascend into an added receptacle. This could be a cap which was a small skep of about 9 in. internal diameter and about 7 in. internal depth. Alternatively a glass bell-jar was used covered by a cap the same size as the hive, for protection and warmth. Although many bell-jars had a ventilating rod down the centre, one finds that unless they are kept well covered not only with a cap but with other surrounding packing also, there is a tendency for condensation to occur.

Neither of these two methods provided much space for storage, and a popular system known as storefying was commonly adopted. In modern terms the hive was supered, in that a skep the same size as the hive, and referred to as a duplet, was placed on it. This too had an aperture in the apex which could be covered with a straw mat if a further super, a triplet, was not to be added. In any case the usual practice in adding a triplet was to place it under the duplet, and there was access by the bees from one super to the other. No queen excluder was used and the queen could, therefore, have access. By the time the duplet and triplet were removed in the autumn it was improbable there would be much if any brood in them, however.

Despite the avoidance of destroying bees under the depriving system not all beekeepers favoured it. The most notable illustration of this was Pettigrew's strong view in the mid 19th century in favouring the single hive. He favoured one of 18 in. internal diameter, or even of 20 in. Depth was 12 in. internal measurement. Moreover he even added an eke or imp on occasions to give still more capacity. This was an extension comprising three or four coils of straw knit to the same diameter as the hive, and added beneath it.

Running contrary to Pettigrew's policy we find, a century earlier, Thomas Wildman's dislike of the single hive, and an abhorrence of the killing of bees. In his opinion a hive of two pecks capacity, a usual size, was too large, and even this was less than half the capacity of that favoured by Pettigrew. He recommended one holding one peck only, being 7 in. deep and 10 in. diameter.

This hive was made in the form of an open-ended straw ring, across one end of which five strips of wood 1 in. wide were laid ½ in. apart. These were plastered firmly into position with cow dung or cloam, and over them a straw cover matching the diameter of the hive was laid, again plastered, and preferably stitched into position. The bars had melted wax run along them, so that a swarm run into the hive would build comb along their length.

In favourable weather conditions a second hive, of the same size, and prepared as the first one but without a top covering, was placed underneath. Subsequent hive additions were made in the same manner, always under the previous one added. In the autumn the upper hives containing honey could be removed, provided the remaining hive contained at least 20 lbs of honey which was considered to be the amount required for winter.

John Keys, at the end of the 18th century, also favoured a bar hive, but larger than Wildman's being 12 in. internal diameter and 9 in internal height, and having seven bars.

Bar frame hives had earlier been used in Greece, but in a hive tapering outwards from base to top, in which bees did not attach comb to the side, so that the combs could be lifted out by the top bars. Here in bar frame hives we see the first tentative thoughts towards a movable comb hive.

Another beekeeper adopting the principle of bars to which bees could attach their comb, was Rev. James Isaac of Devon in the early 19th century. He used what was called the Moreton hive of 12 in. internal diameter and 6 in. internal depth, providing a capacity very little more than that of Thomas Wildman. Again storefying was the practice, but in no storefying system was the queen confined to any one section of a hive unit, meaning that much of any comb containing honey had contained brood, and often still contained brood in one or more sections. *(See Fig. 51).*

As an alternative to adding an eke beneath his hives Pettigrew sometimes added a nadir, which was at least twice the depth of the eke. The principle was the same, in that the hive was appreciably deepened by the addition, and the bees extended their comb downwards into the extra space.

A somewhat similar idea was adopted by James Roberts of Devon in the early 19th century when he produced his Remunerator and Preserver. *(See Fig. 52).* This comprised two parts, the Preserver which was almost globe shaped, and the Remunerator which was a relatively tall skep tapering outwards from the base, and upon which the Preserver stood. The Preserver which was the brood chamber brings to mind Charles Butler's belief that bees were best housed in a hive which was as near as possible to the shape of a globe or sphere. It was, however, appreciably less in capacity being 11 in. wide at the mid part, 7 in. at the base and 9 in. high, all being internal measurements.

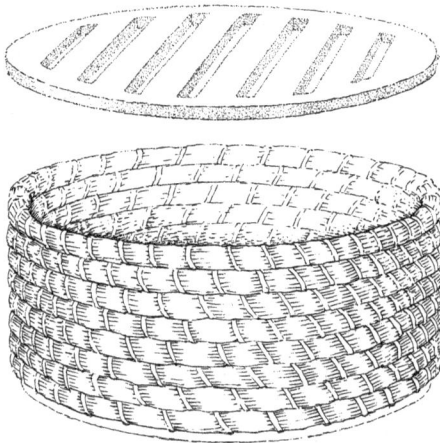

Fig. 51   Moreton Hive.

The Remunerator stood some 15 in. high, about 12 in. internal diameter at the base and about 2 in. wider at the top. It contained two entrances, a normal skep entrance at the base and a further one in the top about two inches from the rim. The Preserver stood on a circular base which had a chamfered entrance coinciding with the top entrance of the Remunerator. When a swarm had become established in the Preserver the bees, under favourable conditions, extended down into the Remunerator and built comb there for storage. The queen would be very unlikely to descend into the Remunerator.

In autumn the Preserver was moved forward so that the circular wooden base upon which it stood covered the Preserver's top entrance. Bees could no longer use this entrance, and came out of the Remunerator by the bottom one and entered the Preserver. Thus clearance took place. Having had the Remunerator cleared it was removed, and not having contained brood, the comb could be expected to be an attractive product. Although I have seen a hive of this type I have not seen it used, but my feeling is that a strong early swarm followed by good weather conditions would be essential to get good build-up so that bees would build down into the Remunerator, and would need to have nectar flowing for work in comb building there, otherwise one can imagine further swarms being encouraged.

Fig. 52   Remunerator and Preserver hive.

Whereas the movable comb hive came into being in 1851 beekeepers in Britain did not promptly forsake the straw hive. Pettigrew in particular continued to strongly favour straw, and it is interesting to find that George Neighbour & Sons in their catalogue for 1871 had by no means discarded straw hives, and even appear to have tried to portray their straw hives in a favourable light in the new beekeeping era, by giving a caption to their skep-hive section which read "Improved Bee-Hives for taking honey without the destruction of the Bees."

69

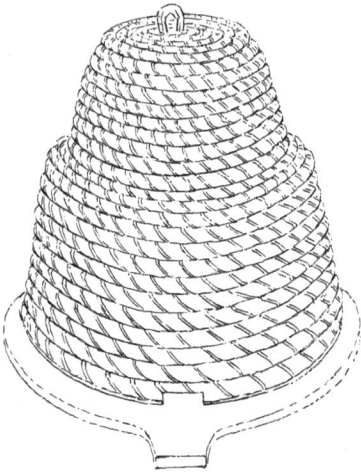

Fig. 53 Common Cottager's Hive
with cap.

A Common Cottager's Hive
comprising a straw depriving hive
with a cap and wooden floor board
was priced at 5s. 6d. and described
as 'Of the simplest form, on the
humane system, intended for the
use of the poor. Is recommended to
the notice of the clergy, and others
interested in the welfare of the
labouring classes'. A more elabor-
ate and expensive hive was the Im-

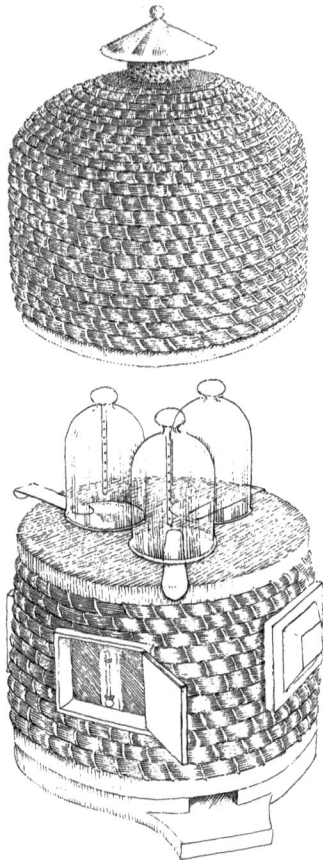

Fig. 54 Neighbour's Improved
Cottage Hive.

proved Cottage Hive priced at £1. 15s. The description given in the
catalogue provides full details of the hive and the use of it and reads as
follows:–

"The Hive is strongly and neatly made, combining the advantages of
a rustic appearance with facilities for inspecting the progress of the bees.
It has three windows in the lower hive, with a thermometer affixed to the
centre one to indicate the temperature of the interior, and thus show
when additional room should be given by admitting the bees into the
glasses. When these glasses are filled with pure honey, they can be taken
away at the most vigorous period of the gathering season, without the

Fig. 55   Woodbury Straw Bar and Frame Hive.

destruction of the bees. Reference to the engraving will show that both the upper and lower hive are made of straw, strengthened with hoops that fit close to the wood. A brass hinge fastens the lower hive to the bottom board, whilst the hoop of the upper hive drops over the crown board, so that the hive is kept firm. The stock hive is not to be interfered with after the swarm is placed therein, and the glass supers are for depri- vation. The upper hive fits over these glasses and may be conveniently raised for inspection. The zinc ventilator on the top allows heated air to pass from the interior. The Improved Cottage Hive has been in extensive use for many years, and has been thoroughly tried. It has had a larger

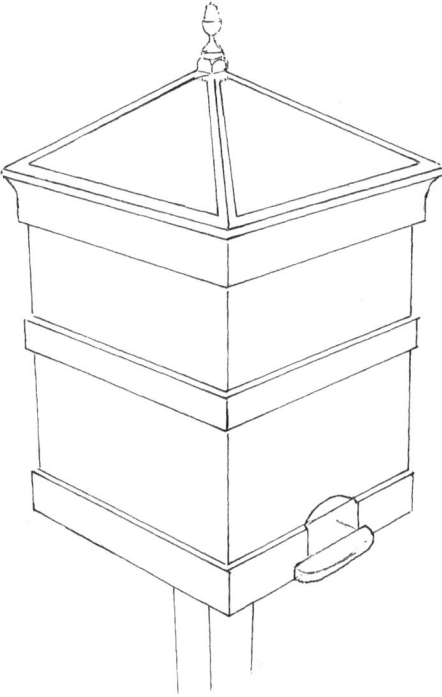

Fig. 56 Outside cover for Woodbury bar and frame hive.

sale, and is more generally approved of than any other Cottage Hive. The simplicity of the arrangements, easy management, combined with tasteful and ornamental appearance render it an especial favourite. Dr Cumming, The Times Beemaster, when describing this hive in his work on Bees and Bee-Hives says 'I have had one of these hives in use for ten years, and it is now as good as when it was new.' Placed either singly or in a row, this unique hive will prove to be a great addition to the flower garden."

Although the catalogue does not say so, bees could be excluded from, or admitted to, the bell jars by metal slides covering apertures in the crown board of the hive. The jars could well be flat topped and with perpendicular sides as distinct from bell shaped. Neighbour & Sons had three sizes of these jars which when filled contained either 10 lbs, 5 lbs or 2 lbs.

Also at this time Neighbour & Sons were manufacturing a square wooden hive holding ten movable frames, to the design of T. W. Woodbury of Devon, the hive being known as The Woodbury Bar and Frame Hive. *(See Fig. 55)*. However, such was the strong feeling still, in favour of straw as a hive material that they manufactured the same hive with straw sides as an alternative to wood. These sides had the appearance of straw matting and were made by tying lengths of straw together in exactly the same manner as in the making of a straw hackle as shown in *Fig. 11*. The sides could be plain or there might be a window built into one of them. A complete hive comprising a stock box, a super, and an outside cover and stand was marketed at £3.

Chapter 8

SWARMS AND HIVE PREPARATION

It is true to say that a good deal of modern beekeeping time and effort is occupied in swarm prevention and control. It is equally true to say that a good deal of the skeppist's time and effort was taken up in encouraging the early swarm and watching for its emergence.

Even those favouring a large hive hoped to obtain good early swarms. To encourage early swarming it was not unusual for beekepers to unite driven bees to other colonies in the autumn. Pettigrew commonly followed this procedure. For the skeppist the benefits of swarming as opposed to non-swarming were the obtaining of clean new comb, the spur which an empty hive gave to the bee, and the natural re-queening of the parent stock.

Hiving swarms on the parent stand does not seem to have been the general practice, and although a first cast if early in the season was usually acceptable, reference to subsequent ones also, by skep day writers, certainly indicates that the parent hive stayed on its own site.

In the 19th century, however, we find reference to artificial swarming of skep bees, and changing the site of the parent stock was then practised. The method was to drive the bees from a strong stock, and when the queen was seen entering the receiver hive this was stood slightly to one side of the parent hive, and this latter was also set slightly to one side of the old stand so that with about 3 feet separating the two it was hoped that each would get an equal number of flying bees returning from foraging. If sufficient bees were not left in the parent hive the remaining bees were driven out also and the receiver hive was then stood on the parent stand, the parent hive being moved to the site of another strong hive which in turn was moved to another position.

Not having the facility of being able to examine a skep colony, but needing to have swarms, and certainly not to lose them, an experienced beekeeper was able to anticipate the emergence by behaviour and weather, but he still kept careful daily watch.

When a swarm was seen to emerge, custom was that of tanging, beating one metal object with another. A large key was often used on a pan, or sometimes on a plough-share. Any clanging noise was supposed to induce a swarm to settle, and there was a belief that the use of the heavy key and plough-share had a special attraction to the swarm.

Little credence can be attached to this belief, in that although vibrations from the tanging could possibly be detected by the bees, it is in the natural order of swarming bees to settle reasonably nearby in any case. However, the swarm could conceivably settle on a neighbour's property, and the clanging did serve to announce the issue and help the owner to lay claim to his valuable swarm.

To quote Charles Butler: "When the swarm is up, and busie in their dance it is a common use, for want of other musicke, to play them a fit of mirth with a pan, kettle, bason, or candlesticke, or other like instrument, so to stay them forsooth from flying away. Indeed where other bee-folds are not far off, this hath a good use, for thereby the place and time of their rising is publikely notified, and so a just and open claim laid unto the swarm, that otherwise some false neighbour might challenge for his which undoubtedly was the original cause for this custome. But the pretended reason is to me a meere fancie, although I know it to be as ancient as common."

King Alfred decreed that "every beekeeper must announce the issue of a swarm by ringing bells or clashing metals so that it might be followed and captured."

Careful preparation of hives which swarms were to occupy was almost a ritual. A new hive was carefully trimmed to remove loose straw and ends, likely to be irritants to the bees. Sometimes the interior was swinged and then rubbed around with a sandstone. This done the interior was rubbed with herbs such as hyssop, thyme, or marjoram. Broad bean tops were often used. Many beekeepers finally rubbed in dilute honey.

Apart from spleeting, the hive was now ready to receive the swarm. Spleets were usually inserted cross-wise, about mid-way down the side. Prior to this preparation it was often the practice to stand a new hive on a board with another board laid across it. Thereon a weight of 56 lbs was placed, which in the language of the skeppists was to 'settle it in a close state' meaning that the hive should sit down well onto the hive base. It was usual to leave the weight in position for about two days. A hive which had been used previously was cleaned as well as possible, to remove old comb and adhering wax prior to being treated with herbs and spleeted, in the same way as a new hive.

Charles Butler described what one must regard as being both needless and unhygienic by saying: "After you have pared away the wax as clean as may be, then let a hogge eat two or three handfuls of mault, or pease, or other corn in the hive, meanwhile do you so turn the hive that the fome or froth which the hogge maketh in eating may go all about the hive. And then wipe the hive lightlie with a linen cloth, and so will the bees like this hive better than new."

As to collecting a swarm Charles Butler again makes a strange, but to some pleasant, suggestion which was that the hiver, wearing no offensive apparel should first drink the best beer and wet his face and hands therewith. The quantity of beer to be consumed was not likely to be enough to make our hiver merry it seems, in that Butler goes on to say "then let him go about his business soberly and gently."

It was not until late in the 19th century that a bellows smoker became part of a beekeeper's equipment, and until then it was hoped that a swarm could be either shaken into a skep, or that it might be on a branch which the beekeeper could sever with the swarm attached. Otherwise it was necessary to brush the bees into the skep. Brushing them downwards was usually much easier than trying to get them to move upwards into the skep by pushing part of their cluster towards the inside of the skep, using either a brush or bundle of twigs, in the hope that the whole swarm would naturally begin to move up into the relative darkness. If the swarm was a late one it would either be run back into the parent hive removing the queen as they did so, or it would be united to an established stock.

The method of uniting was to sprinkle both swarm and stock with thin syrup or dilute honey and then shake out the swarm in front of the stock hive, again removing the queen as the swarm entered the hive.

A British Beekeepers' Association pamphlet on skep beekeeping published soon after 1874, interestingly at a price of one penny, burst Butler's bubble in saying: "Do not in any case wash the hive with anything, sugar, beer, treacle, all are alike – worse than useless."

Nevertheless the fact that attention was drawn to the practice suggests that it was a habit still kept to by some. Old habits among beekeepers often die hard, even now. The same pamphlet described how the skeppist could hope to get the best results. The recommended hive was a depriving one with a 3 in. diameter aperture in the flat crown, having a 15 in. external diameter and being 7 in. to 9 in. depth. A further suggestion was that a wooden hoop be worked on the lower edge to give it strength. This was not by any means a new idea, and had certainly been adopted at the beginning of the 18th century when hazel or willow was fashioned into a hoop with holes burnt through to take the binding. Strength, I suggest, is a secondary purpose, the real one in my opinion

Fig. 57 Section Super and Roof, in position on a hive.

being to extend the life of the hive by protecting the rim from wear and wetness.

The leaflet describes a wooden super for use with this hive, accommodating eighteen 1 lb. sections, and having a wooden roof. *(See Fig. 57).*

Construction can very easily be carried out as shown in the illustrations. *(See Fig. 58).* The super takes the form of a 15½ in. square box, 8½ in. deep in ¾ in. timber to fit over the 15 in. diameter hive. At a depth of 4⅝ in. inside the super an adapter board 15½ in. square and ¼ in. thickness is fixed to four corner blocks firmly glued and screwed in position. This adapter board has a 3 in. diameter hole to correspond with the aperture in the crown of the hive.

To accommodate the sections the modifications are to fix two boards 4⅝ in. deep, parallel to two opposite sides of the super at a distance of 13 in apart. A third board of the same depth and 13 in. long is fixed within 1½ in. of a third wall, and a fourth one of the same size is cut to hold the sections firmly in position. This fourth board is held in position with movable wedges so that the sections can be easily positioned and removed.

Bee space is provided under the sections by fixing battens ¾ in. wide and ⅜ in. deep on the adapter board. These must permit the movable fourth board to close up to the sections, and the centre ones should provide space for bees to have access under the sections from the centre row to the outside ones. Metal dividers are placed between each set of three sections, and a piece of queen excluder is placed over the aperture in the adapter board prior to the sections being assembled.

Over the sections is laid a quilt, and then blanketing or other warm material. The spaces between the section casing and the walls of the super can be filled with chopped straw, and when the roof is in position warmth is well conserved within the super.

76

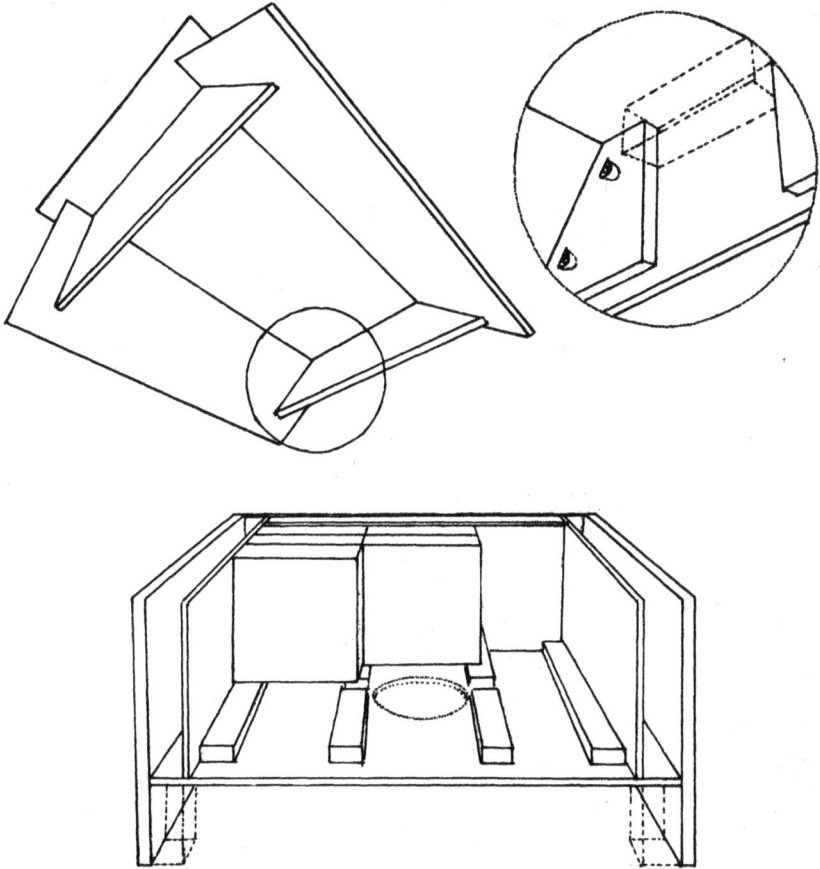

Fig. 58 Construction of section super and roof.

The roof also is made with ¾ in. timber and is simply constructed as shown in the illustration. There is no absolute necessity for the roof to be covered with roofing felt, but this would undoubtedly extend its life.

Apart from use in accommodating sections, this equipment can very conveniently be used to ensure that a skep colony is kept dry and warm throughout the inactive months of autumn and winter.

In late summer feeders are easily positioned over the aperture of the adapter board, and subsequently the uncovered aperture allows good through ventilation during the ensuing months until the spring. The full cost of making this super roof out of new timber is little more than half the cost of purchase from suppliers of a National super, section rack, and hive roof. If one has the odd old hive or other used timber the cost can be very little.

Many beekeepers will be very sceptical as to whether this method of obtaining a surplus is a good one. Certainly obtaining good sections is far from easy under any circumstances, and seems to be a gift rather than a skill. However, in a good summer a strong early swarm can give good results under this method, and even later strong swarms in heather districts can be rewarding.

The names given to swarms over the years have been many, often varying between localities. A rathe swarm was one rising early in the year, and the first swarm from a particular hive was a prime or plum swarm. so that a rathe prime or plum swarm was the skeppist's ideal. Subsequent swarms rising after the prime swarm from any one hive were:–

Second – a cast or castling.

Third – a colt, spindle, hob or hub, smart, foolish.

Fourth – a filly, spew, squib, silver.

A swarm from a swarm of the same year, which was not uncommon, was usually referred to as a maiden swarm, or alternatively a virgin swarm. A swarm rising in late July or even in August was termed a blackberry swarm. Another description of late swarming was wing swarm, but a more likely interpretation of the name is that it referred to a swarm on the wing, taking off to the selected home.

Chapter 9

FEEDING

Prior to the importation of sugar there was no substitute for honey with which to feed. It was, therefore, essential in those days to ensure that a colony had sufficient natural stores upon which to winter. At the end of the season, when considering which hives to lift it was customary for the beekeeper to decide to lift the lightest and the heaviest, leaving those of medium weight for wintering, but it was essential to ensure that these wintering hives were of 20 lbs total weight at the very least, and more if the combs were known to be old.

Hefting was a skill in itself, and a practice to be conscientiously performed. Keys made a survey of winter food consumption and found in one mild winter from 2nd November to 27th February that the weight loss was 5 lb 2 oz over the 115 days, about ¾ oz per day. As to material for feeding, sugar being available in his day, he found none more successful, cheap, or convenient than soft brown sugar dissolved in mild ale in the proportion of one pound to half a pint. He conceded to the feeding of honey if sugar was dear.

His method of feeding was with troughs made from joints of elder, angelica, or kecks. These joints were cut to about 8 in. in length, split to form a trough and flattened on the underside. The pith was removed and the ends were plugged. When filled these troughs were pushed under the combs in the evening, and re-filled the following evening. They held about ¾ oz, which seems to be a totally inadequate amount for autumn feeding, and likely to do little more than encourage the queen to continue laying.

Not only do we find a controversial food having been recommended, but Keys also quotes a controversial policy of feeding, by saying that in 1777 he fed daily during the winter which was a mild one, two very light stocks through the dreary season until the end of May. Using a thick syrup made from ale and brown sugar he reports that the bees survived and flourished. He called this private feeding, and affirmed that since the bees were prevented from feeding to excess they avoided a looseness which occurred when an abundant supply was given at once. Public feeding was also decribed by Keys. In the absence of nectar being available, a comb was filled on one side with his honeyed ale, and openly placed in the apiary. Spring feeding he favoured, to stimulate and encourage early breeding.

The idea of providing food daily through the winter, as described by Keys, must raise a lot of eyebrows. He did say that the winter was mild, but as a policy one can hardly go along with his reasoning.

I have, however, fed bees through the winter myself with no ill effects to them, and indeed I found the end result quite successful. On 11th November I had visited a farm in mid Devon to inspect a set of bee boles. Over a welcome cup of tea the farmer's wife told me they had a colony of bees in an upturned sheep trough and they wanted to be rid of them. The following day I went back to the farm equipped with a travelling box and a carving knife. Having carefully cut through the fragile comb attachments I propped the various pieces in my box and journeyed home.

It was obvious that I could do nothing at that time of the year to establish the colony in a permanent home and I, therefore, covered the box with waterproofing to at least keep the colony dry. Judging by the amount of virgin comb and number of bees there was little doubt that the small colony had developed from a late cast. It had no more than about 2 lbs of food so a small block of candy was propped as near to the cluster as possible.

On 14th November, two days after arrival at my apiary pollen was being carried into the new home, and indeed continued to be carried on any good flying day throughout the winter. I opened the box about every fourteen days to give a fresh small cake of candy if necessary. In all to the end of January 5 lbs of candy were given. On 5th February I was able to position an accessible feeder near to the cluster and fed 2 lbs of thick syrup, continuing to give similar amounts at intervals until the end of March. By this time a substantial amount of new comb had been built and the colony was growing quickly.

In mid April it was possible to establish the colony in a skep hive. Not only did these spartans survive but they prospered in spite of being frequently disturbed and fed. Had the winter not been a mild one I may well have had a different story to tell.

It was during the 18th century that sugar, in any quantity, began to be imported into Britain, and even then only the more well-to-do could afford it, so that although Keys was able to use sugar late in the century, honey would, in all probability, be less expensive than sugar in the early part of the century.

Back in the 17th century and earlier, feeding had to be done with honey. If this was not fed as honey alone in the small shallow troughs, a piece of bruised comb was placed on thin slats of wood enabling the bees to have access to both sides of the comb. The hive was raised and the comb on the slats was positioned beneath it. A more Heath Robinson method was to push spoons filled with honey into the entrance, or alternatively a piece of honeyed toast. If public feeding with honey was done, although it was not a favoured method, honeycomb or honey was placed in the apiary, after having first closed up those hives considered not to need food.

By the mid 19th century commercial feeders were in use for hives with a top aperture, one being a contact feeder comprising a wooden ring with a central hole in which the neck of a glass bottle covered with mesh was placed and the whole was stood over the hive aperture. Others were rapid feeders and took the form of circular containers with a central entry column in the base through which the bees had access to syrup in the surrounding trough. The principle was the same as that of similar present day feeders. They were made of wood, zinc, or earthenware.

It was common, even in the 18th century, to quote the price of honey relative to gallons. In *Evidence of Welsh Beekeeping in the Past* reference is made to records of sales of honey at 5d. per gallon in the mid 13th century and at 10d. per gallon in the mid 14th century. These were periods well before sugar importation.

A more recent reference was made by Dr. John Satchell of Kendal in Cumbria writing in the Westmorland Gazette newspaper, quoting honey and sugar prices in the town during 1719 and 1720. He referred to the household accounts of Benjamin Browne of Troutbeck near Windermere which he discovered in the County Record Office in Kendal. These accounts showed that Benjamin Browne purchased in 1719 and 1720, brandy at 1s. 6d. a quart, brown sugar at 4½d. and 5½d. a pound, loaf sugar at 8½d., and powdered sugar at 1s. a pound. In 1719 the accounts showed an entry for two quarts of honey for two shillings. This volume of honey was equivalent to 7 lbs weight, making the price of honey about 3½d. a pound which was less than the cheapest quotation for brown sugar at 4½d. a pound.

A further illustration of the relative dearness of sugar at that time is seen in the price of brandy at 1s. 6d. a quart, which was no more than the price of 4 lbs of brown sugar. This firm evidence of sugar and honey prices indicates that a beekeper would not wish to have to use sugar for feeding, and his ability in hefting hives to assess the stores in them each autumn was an essential skill.

Present day prices of honey and sugar make an interesting comparison. Honey in Devon is selling for £1.50 per pound in the shops, and sugar costs 24 pence per pound.

Chapter 10

QUIETENING AND FUMIGATING

The need to subdue skep bees did not arise to the same extent as with bees on movable combs in that it was not possible to manipulate skep combs and to perform modern management techniques with skep hives. Nevertheless even Virgil recognised the need on occasions to subdue or quieten bees when he wrote:–

"With sprinkled water first the city choke.
And then pursue the citizens with smoke."

Sprinkling with water, or honeyed water, and in more recent years with very dilute sugar syrup, was a common method of quietening a colony.

It was not until 1875, however, that a satisfactory smoker was perfected. As to how smoke was produced and administered was relatively primitive before this date. One method was to make a roll of corduroy or fustian which was just tight enough to burn. Sometimes tobacco was sprinkled into the roll. Once this torch-like roll was smouldering the beekeeper blew smoke from it into the hive before lifting it and allowing smoke to ascend well up between the combs.

Another method was referred to in John Evelyn's Manuscript on Bees in 17th century. This was the burning of dried cow dung on a chafing dish of burning coal. The fumes from the cow dung were allowed to drift into a hive held over the chafing dish. The beekeeper was advised to also let the fumes drift over his hands and face. Having done this he was able to turn up the hive and look down the combs.

The chafing dish principle and method also served to provide a means of administering, either alone or with dried cow dung, a substance called olibanum. This was a dried oleo-resinous secretion obtained from the bark of Boswellia, a tree indigenous to Southern Arabia. It was recommended by Edmunde Southerne at the end of the 16th century in *Treatise Concerning the Right Use and Ordering of Bees*, that at about the latter end of March if bees "appeared to go but slowly out and in" olibanum should be used to enable the bees to "abide the sharpness of the weather the better."

Fig. 59   Roman earthenware Smoker.

The method of use was to bruise a little of the olibanum with a pestle and mortar, and to scatter the substance on a chafing dish of burning coal. Dried cow dung could be added if the beekeeper wished to do so.

The hive being treated was held over the chafing dish. The fragrant volatile oil contained in the olibanum is used as an ingredient of incense, an alternative name being frankincense which was one of the gifts of the wise men to the infant Jesus. How wise the skeppists were in using it may now seem somewhat doubtful to us.

An alternative to olibanum was galbanum referred to by D. A. Smith in editing John Evelyn's *Manuscript on Bees*, and by Herrod Hempsall. This also was an odiferous resin administered in the same way. John Evelyn said that, whilst the perfume "delights and profits the bees", it should not be used for more than two minutes at a time.

Herrod Hempsall refers to the use of it by the Romans when it was used in an earthenware vessel in which were numerous perforations *(See Fig. 59)*. The mellarius or beekeeper blew into the open end of the vessel and directed the fumes coming from the perforations onto the bees. Columella said "Though it be troublesome to the hive yet it is considered exceeding wholesome".

The forerunners of our modern bellows smoker, although far from being satisfactory, were roughly on the same principle. One was an ordinary briar pipe which had a rubber tube, plugged at one end, placed over the bowl of the pipe once the tobacco in the pipe was alight. The rubber tube was then alternatively pressed and released to provide smoke from

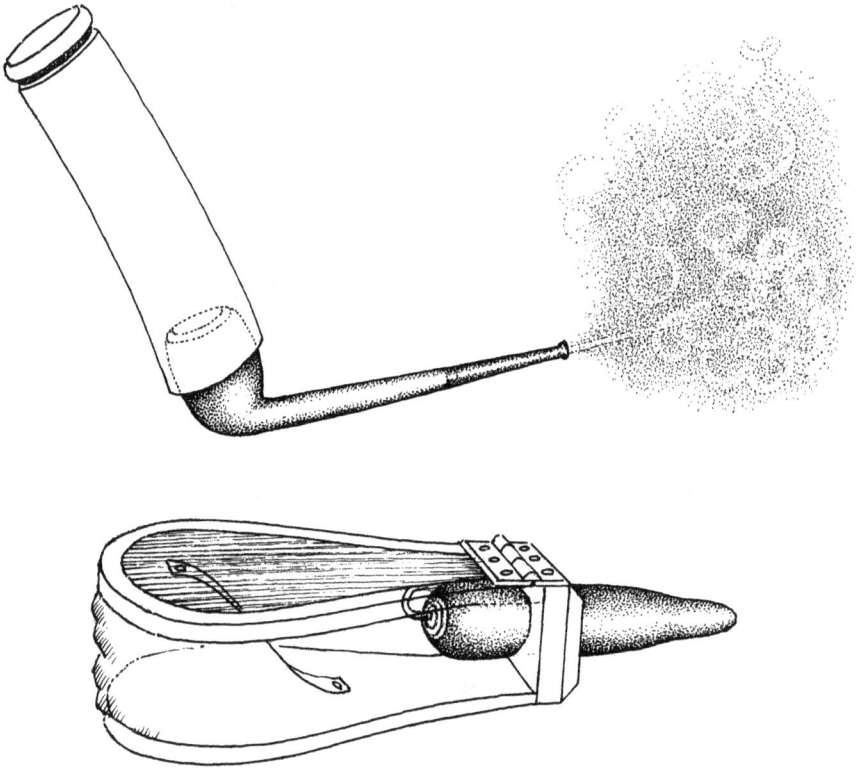

Fig. 60   Early smokers.

the stem *(See Fig. 60)*. This simple invention was credited to F. Cheshire.

At about the same time Rev. H. Bligh invented a smoker with bellows. The container was charged with tobacco or maybe woollen material, the smoke from which was ejected by the bellows through the nozzle *(See Fig. 60)*. Occasionally a puff-ball was burnt if it was intended to stupefy the bees rather than to merely subdue them.

Neither Mr Cheshire's pipe nor Rev Bligh's bellows smoker provided very much smoke, and it would not seem likely that either of these pieces of equipment would be much help in swarm collection. For other purposes, since smoke was not as essential as with the movable comb hive, the volume would be adequate. In my opinion some modern beekeepers tend to be far too free with the smoker, and many is the time that bees are being irritated by billowing smoke rather than being quietened by a gently drifting puff of it.

Chapter 11

THE MASTER SKEPPIST

To some Pettigrew may well have been regarded, not so much as the master skeppist, but as the most stubborn, and when we read in his Handy Book of Bees that he would not accept as a gift the hives of wood being invented at the time we might well feel that he was being just too unreasonable. His reasons for preferring straw hives and his methods of skep beekeeping are not only fascinating to look into, but enlightening also, showing good reason for his beliefs.

As to hives Pettigrew declared:– "Straw hives, well sewed with split canes or bramble-briers, are incomparably better for bees than any other kind of hive yet introduced. Nothing better is needed, and we believe nothing better will ever be found out." Strong words indeed. His reasons for preferring straw to wood were because of cheapness, neatness and lightness. Hardly sufficient reasons to outweigh wood, but he did, in my opinion, appreciate that wood at certain times of the year condenses moisture from the colony which causes deterioration of the comb. He might well have gone on to say that straw was absorbant, and that the round shape of the skep hive conforming to the shape of the winter cluster helped to conserve cluster warmth.

Still defending straw he linked large size to his argument by saying:– "To have done let me again say that well made straw hives of considerable dimensions are better than wood hives of any description, better for the swarming system of management, and better for the non-swarming, better for comb building, and better for honey gathering, better for health, and better for ventilation, equal in every way to wood for supers, better for nadirs, better for winter and better for summer."

By considerable dimensions Pettigrew meant between 16 in. and 20 in. internal diameter, the type of hive being the common hive. This size of hive was the basis of Pettigrew's methods. He inserted cross sticks inside the hives to support the combs. These cross sticks were sometimes referred to as spleets, and five or six of them were inserted in every hive to run from side to side. *(See Fig. 61)*. Guide combs were used in the hives to ensure that comb was built running from back to front of the hive and at

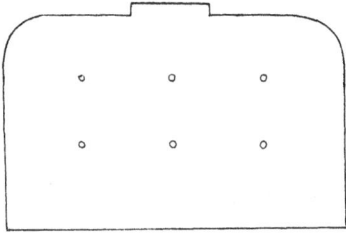

Fig. 61 Diagram of hive showing position of cross sticks.

right angles to the cross sticks. The diagram shows the positioning of sticks, the bottom row of which was to be at least 4 in. above the floor board. The bees built the comb round them but often left pop holes where the sticks passed through the comb. Guide combs were small pieces of comb about 2 in. square and were fixed to thin slivers of wood which were then fastened to the crown of the hive. This spleeting or sticking of hives was not a new idea though earlier beekeepers had variations of the system such as that of Charles Butler with his cop and spleets.

At much the same time as Charles Butler, John Levett advocated a "Crowne Tree". The principle was the same except that no cop was used. A hazel or willow stick, thumb thickness, was quartered down its length until, as Levett says, "about half a handful." This end was sharpened and pushed hard into the top centre of the hive, the quarters then being bent and sharpened to hold into the hive sides about 6 in. above the hive floor. Levett further recommended that two additional sticks be affixed into the hive sides within four fingers of the hive floor.

Pettigrew seemed to have no liking for supers of any kind, always appearing to prefer not only to use a large hive but to extend the size still further by the use of an eke consisting of about four coils and placed beneath the hive. Alternatively he used a nadir, which was the opposite of a super in that it was placed below a hive whereas a super was placed on the top.

The significance of these two devices was that ekes were used where weight of honey was the aim, and also where it was desired to prevent the issue of a swarm. Nadirs were used where the aim was to get weight of honey, and still be left with the stock. What happened in nadiring was that if a hive which it was intended to keep for stock became heavy in June then an empty hive with cross sticks and an aperture in the crown was placed beneath that stock. It would soon be found that the bees in this strong stock were hanging down into the nadir. In conditions of nectar flow, comb was quickly drawn and brood rearing then took place there. By the end of the season honey would be stored in the top hive and brood be in the lower one. The top one was then removed and the lower one was left for stock.

Where an eke had been added it was improbable that swarming would occur, provided there had been no undue delay in so doing and the colony would be one from which honey could be taken. Pettigrew strongly disapproved of the sulphur pit and drove the bees from such a hive to be united with another colony. Alternatively the driven bees were allowed to run back into their hive after some of the honey in it had been cut out.

Pettigrew was very much in favour of encouraging early top or first swarms. By early he meant May, and certainly no later than very early in June if poor conditions for bees had prevailed. He achieved good wintering strength and early build up to swarming condition by his custom of driving and uniting bees in the autumn. He also favoured making early artificial swarms, a custom which he said his father had adopted early in the 19th century, and which he further said may have been invented by his father.

Briefly Pettigrew's belief was: "For gaining great profits in a favourable year, and for continued prosperity over a number of years the system of having strong hives and early swarms lifts itself up in statuesque form above all the other systems of managing bees. Supers, nadirs and ekes are useful, profitable, and indispensable for hives that require enlarging later in the season. Which is best the bee-master must decide."

Another practice which he often carried out was what he described as a turnout. This was that bees were driven from a swarmed hive three weeks after the event. Such hives frequently contained a good quantity of honey. Obtaining the honey was not the sole consideration, however, since the colony contained a young queen and was ideal to be united with a colony containing an old queen. It also formed part of Pettigrew's sound practice of comb replacement as well as maintaining young queens. No hive, he said, was to be kept for more than two years.

As to the price of swarms in the late 19th century Pettigrew in 1870 said "Beekeeping can be commenced with May or June swarms, or at any time. We sell our first swarms put in good new straw hives with boards for 25 shillings each, without hives and boards for 21 shillings each. Second swarms are 5 shillings each less in price."

Pettigrew's deep seated opinions, honest though they were, gave no concessions whatever to other than skep-hive beekeeping, and almost amounted to complete intolerance of change. "One gentleman," he said, "manufacturer of hives, has written to say that he will give me much information on bees if I will only mention his ten-bar frame hive. Poor fellow." His contemporary, John Hunter, in *A Manual of Beekeeping* expressed a much more reasonable view in saying "I like a skep, it is so nice and handy, and if its interior were not like a sealed book it should have an honoured place in my apiary."

Chapter 12

SKEP BEEKEEPING TODAY

Nobody can seriously suggest a return to skep beekeeping as a commercial enterprise, but to many beekeepers who look for maximum pleasure to themselves and a minimum of stress to the bees, skep beekeeping provides the means. By working with nature in the interests of the bee a skeppist will obtain surplus honey, perform a measure of disease control, give the colony good wintering conditions, and allow it to develop naturally.

Keeping skep hives dry is of primary importance, and to do so the most satisfactory method is to erect a shelter which may be of stone as shown in Appendix I or it may be of timber as shown in the photograph of a lean-to shelter at an apiary in North Yorkshire, where the beekeeper enjoys keeping a few hives to a system closely following that of Pettigrew. *(See Fig. 62)*.

Fig. 62   Lean-to shelter in North Yorkshire.

The hives have apertures in the crown, but are used as single hives to which ekes can be added if this becomes necessary. The aperture is useful should feeding be needed, but it is otherwise kept covered.

The maximum size of hive he uses is approximately 16 in. internal diameter and 12 in. internal height giving about 2400 cubic inches capacity as compared with a National Brood Box of 2150 cubic inches. The method he follows is to hive early swarms, hopefully from the middle to the end of May, into these large hives. They build up strongly through the summer, and are taken to the heather, usually with an eke added. Cross sticks are pushed through the ekes in the same manner as those in the hives. On return from the moors the bees are driven from these hives during the first week in October in the manner illustrated by *Fig. 50*.

The driven bees are then united to another colony by inverting the hive containing them over the mouth of another hive, newspaper being spread between the two. After twenty-four hours the top hive can be removed and the receiving hive be replaced normally, on its stand. After driving, the cross sticks are withdrawn from the hives, and the comb is then cut out. Before driving and uniting a light spray of thin syrup is given to each colony. This beekeeper is rightly concerned that comb must never be allowed to be used for longer than seventeen months, which means that a swarm hived in May must be driven in October of the following year if it was not driven in the October of the year of swarming.

Not every beekeeper will feel confident enough to drive bees, and may also find positioning an eke an inconvenience. A simpler alternative, known as nadiring, which has already been referred to as being favoured on occasions by Pettigrew, can be followed. A suitable size of hive is 14 in. internal diameter and 9 in. internal height having a capacity of about 1400 cubic inches. A swarm in May in a hive of this size can be expected to fully occupy it after four weeks in favourable weather. Another hive of the same size with a 3 in. aperture in the crown is then placed beneath the first hive and stapled to it. Bees in the upper hive soon hang down in a cluster through the crown hole of the lower hive, the nadir. Brood soon appears in comb built in the nadir, and most of the honey is then stored in the upper hive, and can be removed at the end of the season. In a good season it may even be necessary to add a third hive which should be placed under the last one added.

Many beekeepers will be more attracted to supering a skep hive than to using an eke or a nadir. Again the hive to be used must have a 3 in. diameter aperture in the crown, over which a piece of queen excluder is placed. The size of hive to be used is at the beekeeper's own discretion if it is intended to use as a super another skep of the same size. If, as the season progresses, it is desired to enlarge the hive this is done by the method of adding an eke.

Such an occasion would arise if it was thought there was a danger of an unwanted swarm by reason of overcrowding. In a good season a second super is likely to be needed, and should be added beneath the first one. In size it must have the same diameter as the first super and the hive, but need not be of identical depth. There must, of course, be an aperture of 3 in. diameter in the crown of the second super.

It is advisable to fasten supers to each other and to the hive by the use of staples placed at intervals through the straw. Modern hive staples serve very well for this purpose. Instead of using supers of a size matching that of the hive, a smaller skep commonly referred to as a cap can be used, but if a second super became necessary it should be of the same diameter as the hive.

Supering with skeps, as described, is not the only method. A very fascinating one is to use a bell jar if one is fortunate enough to be able to acquire one, or some other kind of glass container the mouth of which will fit over the crown aperture of the hive. Unless the vessel being used has perforations in the manner of bell jars used in skep beekeeping days it is advisable to place thin slips of wood under the lip to give some ventilation. It is essential that such glass containers should be well covered and be wrapped to avoid condensation. A deep skep can be used as a cover, or a hackle serves very well.

Apart from any other advantage of skeps that of cheapness is a distinct attraction. Costs of beekeeping can be a deterrent to many, but having made skep hives at little cost it is quite practicable to use them with adapted wooden supers. One is designed to take section boxes, and another is designed to take standard frames.

In an earlier chapter the making of a section super is described, and although the production of good sections is by no means easy, the making of the super during the winter months offers the challenge of producing sections in the manner they were produced a century ago.

A strong swarm is essential with a good nectar flow following it. We cannot control the weather and nectar flow, but we can ensure, by feeding if necessary, that the swarm is not held back in comb building and brood rearing to take advantage of the flow when it does come. One or two bait sections are undoubtedly an encouragement to the bees to work in the super. Built as described the super has the necessary warmth, but covering the sections with blanketing or a chaff cushion also helps. And why not take a good swarm, well established, to the heather. Transport offers no problems, in that the entrance is easily stopped with foam rubber, and a wire mesh screen can easily be tacked over the super.

To help the stability of the hive on its base I have sometimes fixed four pegs in the form of a square within the circumference of the hive skirt in the base, and this idea helps in transportation. Producing good sections by any method is far from simple, but with a skep hive there is a real fascination in the task.

If working for sections seems to offer too big a challenge then modern shallow frames are very easily used to super a depriving hive. A shallow National super or National brood box are both very simply adapted as illustrated, and are used under a National hive roof.

Shallow Super

An adapter board 18⅛ in. square from ¼ in. board, in the centre of which a 3 in. diameter hole must be cut, is needed. The hole is to correspond with the aperture in the crown of the hive. The board is then fixed on the base of the super which must have bottom bee space. Fixing need only be with a few panel pins.

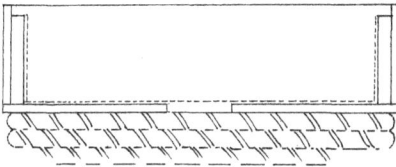

Fig. 63 National shallow super with adapter board.

This super should be used on a hive having an external diameter of 18 in, and if the internal height was 10 in. the hive capacity would approximate to that of a National brood box *(See Fig. 63)*. Apart from having an adapter board lightly pinned to the base the super has not been altered and can be brought back into use with a wooden brood box when required. It is not necessary to fasten the super to the hive in any way.

Clearing a super is done in the same manner as clearing a modern hive. If a National hive clearer board is used it should be adapted to allow the board to sit securely on the hive and also prevent robbing and the return of bees to the supers. This is done by fixing a 13 in. square inner frame, of the same thickness and width of wood as the 18⅛ in. square outer frame, to the underside as shown in *Fig. 64.*

If a hive with the same capacity as a National brood box is used then it is probable that further supers will need to be added. They should be placed over the existing one. There need be no anxiety regarding the ability of the hive to carry the weight of the supers provided it is firmly made and with perpendicular sides which do not form a rounded shoulder with the crown.

91

Fig. 64   Adapted clearer board.

Rounded shoulders would mean that the weight was being carried entirely on the crown causing it to sink and to damage comb in the hive. To avoid this danger the sides must commence at an immediate right angle to the crown as described in chapter three.

Brood Box

A brood box can be adapted in exactly the same way as a shallow super, and be furnished with standard brood frames. Alternatively the adapter board can be cut to fit the interior of the brood box and be fixed to battens 2½ in. deep inside the brood box so that there is bottom spacing in the super portion above it. *(See Fig. 65).* In that case, however, the hive would have to be no larger than 14 in. external diameter meaning that its internal diameter would be only 12 in. and give a capacity only about half that of National brood box and for that reason would not be a practical size.

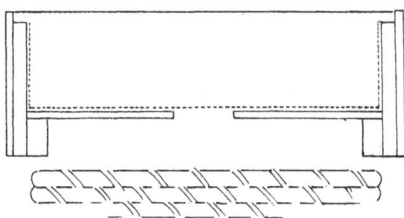

Fig. 65   National brood box with adapter board.

Adapted in the same way as a shallow super it could likewise be used on an 18 in. diameter hive.

A natural thought before enjoying a skep beekeeping venture may well be to wonder if bees are likely to winter satisfactorily in a skep, and how they can, if desired, be transferred to a modern hive. My experiences

92

in wintering skep colonies have been that provided a hive is kept dry the bees fare better than their modern hive neighbours.

If one does not have a shelter then a firm hackle ensures a dry home, and the absence of eight cold corners promotes a warmer one, nearer in shape to that of the clustered tenants. In the harsh winter of 1985/6 I wintered one skep colony. Not only did it survive, whereas half my National colonies succumbed, but spring found it strong and building up quickly in spite of the still severe weather.

In spring, if one wishes, a strong over-wintered skep colony can be introduced to a modern hive filled with frames by merely placing the skep on a division board the size of the particular brood box. The division board must have an aperture of about 4 in. square. In good conditions the colony will soon work down onto the frames. Once the queen is laying well there, queen excluder is placed over the aperture having ensured that the queen is in the brood chamber, and not the skep. The excluder is left in position until all brood in the skep has emerged.

The transfer is now complete and the skep on its board can be removed. If the transfer is being made into a National hive then an adapter board as used under a National hive super on a skep hive is ideal to place between the skep and the National brood chamber.

A criticism of skep hives is that they do not permit proper inspection of the brood for possible disease. With this one must, in the main, agree. Nevertheless it is no great problem on a good flying day to lift a hive, let the sun fall directly down the combs, and part the centre ones somewhat to reveal some brood. A good slab of solidly sealed brood is a fair indication that all is well.

Finally, however, it must be remembered that comb in a skep hive must not be used for longer than two seasons. To ensure this, driving in the autumn is the most practical method, but if a beekeeper cannot acquire the necessary skill to drive the bees then he should adopt the spring transfer onto frames method described above. Another swarm can then be awaited and given its honoured place in your apiary.

Appendix 1

BEE SHELTER CONSTRUCTION

Like the bee bole, the bee shelter is built to no fixed measurements. The basic style is that shelters abut onto a house or garden wall on a lean-to principle.

The example shown illustrates the erection of a shelter onto an existing garden wall, and is based on a known bee shelter in the Lake District. It is illustrated with some of the slates and timbers removed to show the underlying construction. This can be varied to use materials which match the existing wall, and many may prefer a paved floor which is more in keeping than a concrete one. There is only one shelf shown, but a second one can be included above the lower one so that two rows of skeps can be accommodated. If it is intended to use the shelter purely as a summerhouse, only the lower shelf, to be used as a seat, is required.

A suggested size for the shelter is:—
Internal width six feet.
Internal depth three feet.
Front height of buttress five feet.
Rear height of buttress seven feet.

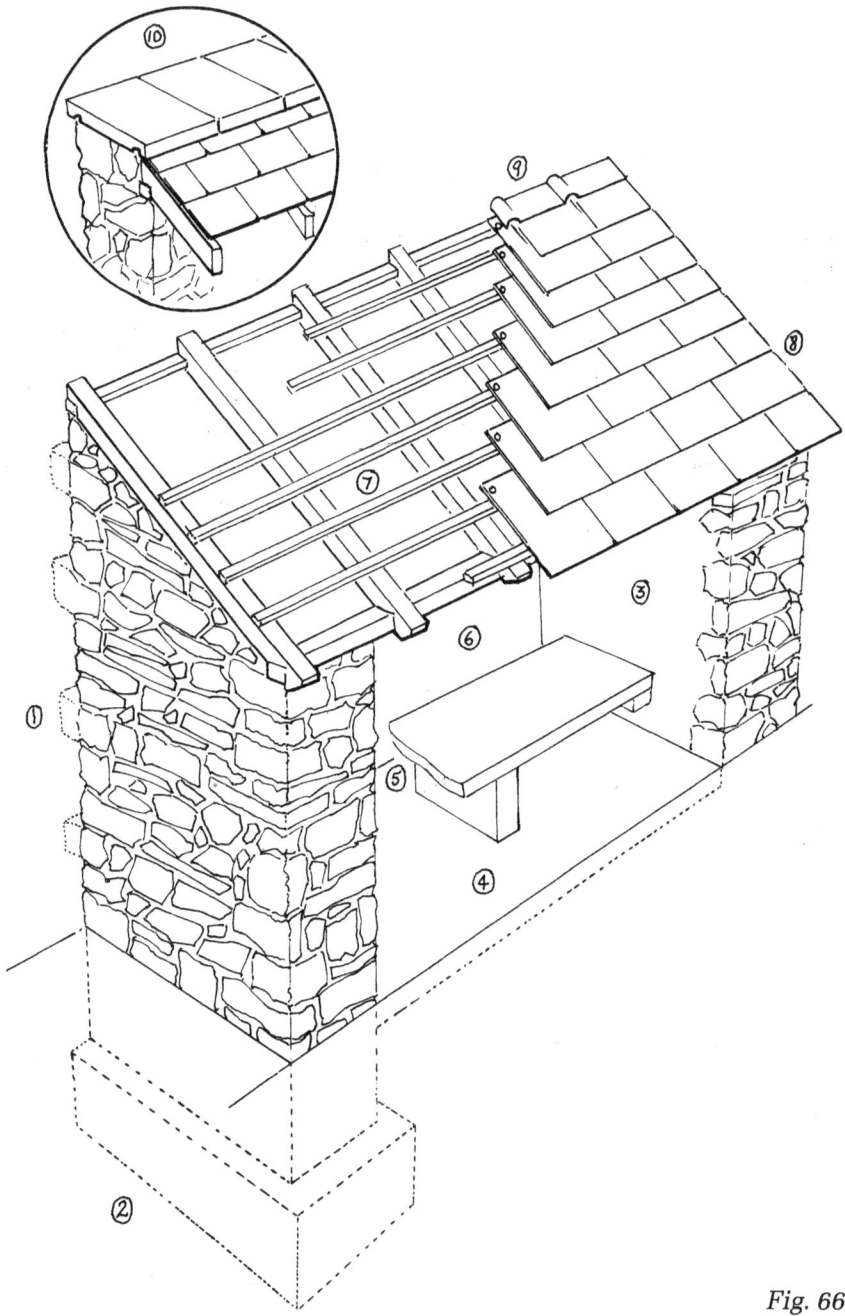

Fig. 66

Fig. 66 BEE SHELTER CONSTRUCTION

KEY NOTES

1. Walls in stonework (random rubble or slate), 18 in. thick keyed into back wall.

2. Foundations, concrete, 6 in. thick, preferably not less than 18 in. deep.

3. Inner face can be plastered and should have projections to support shelves 18 in. or more wide.

4. The floor should be 4 in. thick concrete on hardcore base with an even surface 2 in. above ground level and sloping to the front for drainage.

5. Shelves may be of wood, slate or reinforced concrete slabs supported clear of the floor and back wall to allow air circulation.

6. The roof is supported by a 3 in. x 4 in. purlin at the front and a 2 in. x 4 in. wall plate fixed to the wall at the rear.

7. 4 in. x 2 in. joists at up to 18 in. centres are notched to the purlin and plate and carry 1½ in. x 1½ in. battens to which the slates are nailed.

8. A wide variety of slates may be used and these are laid to courses with suitable laps to cover joints and nails. The eaves course is usually doubled or tilted to ensure the slate edges close up.

9. The ridge of the roof may be covered by special ridge tiles, or if it is level with the top of the wall, stone copings may be used to cover both the wall and the upper edge of the roof. *(See Fig. 66, inset 10).*

Appendix 2

BEEKEEPING MUSEUMS
AND PLACES WITH ITEMS OF INTEREST

1. I.B.R.A. Collection of Historical and Contemporary Beekeeping Material at International Bee Research Association, 16 North Road, Cardiff, CF1 3DY. Viewing by appointment only. Office hours Monday to Friday, 9 a.m. to 5.30 p.m., except Bank Holidays. Tel. (0222) 372409.

2. Scottish Agricultural Museum. Royal Highland Showground, Ingliston, near Edinburgh. Open 1st May to 30th September, 10.00 a.m. to 5 p.m., Monday to Friday and on Sundays from 12 noon to 5 p.m. Group visits year round by appointment. Tel. 031-557 3550.

3. Welsh Folk Museum. St. Fagans, Cardiff. CF5 6XB. Open Monday to Saturday 10 a.m. to 5 p.m. and on Sundays from 2.30 p.m. to 5 p.m. Beekeeping material is in Department of Farming and Rural Life. Tel. (0222) 569311.

4. Cotswold Countryside Collection, Northleach, Cheltenham, Glos. GL54 3JH. Open daily April to October. Monday to Saturday 10 a.m. to 5.30 p.m., Sundays 2 p.m. to 5.30 p.m. Tel. (04516) 715. Skepmaking by D. Chubb, of Box Bush Farm, South Cerney, Glos. may, at certain times, be seen there. Enquiries for times.

5. Bicton College of Agriculture. East Budleigh, Devon. A few interesting historical beekeeping items may be seen there by special appointment. Tel. (995) 68353.

GLOSSARY

ALVEARY a small conical wicker hive.

BEE BOLE a recess in a wall to accommodate a straw bee hive.

BEO CEORL in the Old English constitution a low ranking freeman with the responsibility of beekeeping.

BENNETS long coarse grasses, rushes, or sedges.

BYKE or BIKE a nest of wild bees in a hollow tree or log.

CHAFING DISH vessel to hold burning charcoal or other fuel for heating anything upon it.

CLOAM, CLOOM or CLOOME cow dung mixed with ashes, lime, sand or gravel.

COB a composition of clay, gravel, and straw, used in the South West of England for building walls during 16th and 17th centuries in particular.

COP the head, top, or summit of anything, described by Rev Charles Butler as being a round block of wood fitting into the top of a straw hive to hold spleets.

COPPET a cap or cover, an alternative name for a hackle.

CREAMER a dish used in small dairies for settling milk and having a capacity of six quarts. Earthenware, narrow at base, widening to the top.

EKE a short cylinder of straw, other reed, or wood on which a hive can be placed to increase its capacity.

EORL in the Old English constitution a man of noble rank, as distinguished from a ceorl or ordinary freeman.

GARTH a small piece of enclosed land usually beside a house. Also an alternative to gart.

GART a wooden hoop as for a barrel, or to place round a hackle covering a straw hive. Sometimes called a garth.

HACKLE an outer garment, also long shining feathers on the neck of certain birds. Was used to describe the protective straw covering placed over common hives.

HONEY-POKE a small bag through which honey was strained.

KECK, KECKS, KESH, or KEX name given to both Cow Parsley and Cow Parsnip. Large hollow stemmed Umbelliferae. Names vary in different localities, e.g. Kesh in Lakeland, parts of Yorkshire and Lancashire. Other local names are Queen Anne's lace and lady's needlework.

LACINGS strips of hazel or willow used for binding reed in skep-making.

LISSOM a coil of reed in skep-making.

NADIR in beekeeping another part added to a hive below the existing part, similar to an eke but deeper.

NEAT a working animal of the ox tribe.

NITCHE, NITCH, NICHE, NETCH, or NUTCH a definite quantity of hay, straw or reeds. A nitche of reeds for thatching weighs 36 lbs, though a half or even a quarter of this quantity is usual.

PANCHEON a name used in Yorkshire and other parts of Northern England for a creamer used in small dairies.

RUSKY or RUSKIE in Scotland a skep, but may also be any utensil made of straw or reed.

SKEP originally used for bee hives, but is more widely a basket made of straw or other reed, and is derived from skeppa a Scandinavian word.

SMIT a mark of ownership put on sheep. About 600 varieties of smit and lug mark exist in the English Lake District.

SPLEET a small strip of split wood or willow.

STOREFYING or STORIFYING in skep beekeeping days used to describe supering.

SULPHURING the old barbaric custom of killing bees by placing hives over burning sulphur.

TANGING an old custom of making a loud noise by banging metal objects together announcing the issue of a swarm, supposedly encouraging it to settle.

BIBLIOGRAPHY

Alphabetical Guide for Beekeepers. K. C. Stevens, 1985.

The Archaeology of Beekeeping. E. Crane, 1983.

Beekeeping New and Old described with pen and camera. Vol 1 and Vol 2. W. Herrod Hempsall, 1930 and 1937.

Beeswax. R. H. Brown, 1981.

Cumberland and Westmorland Beekeepers' Association Year Book, 1906.

English Bee Boles. E. Crane and R. M. Duruz, 1953.

John Evelyn's Manuscript on Bees from Elysium Britannicum. D. A. Smith, 1966.

Evidence on Welsh Beekeeping in the Past. E. Crane and P. Walker, 1985.

The Feminine Monarchie. Charles Butler, 1609.

The Handy Book of Bees. A Pettigrew, 1870.

History of Beekeeping in Britain. H. M. Fraser, 1958.

History and Topography of Westmorland and Cumberland. Nicholson and Burn, 1776.

Hogs at the Honeypot. F. G. Vernon, 1981.

Make your own Skep and revive a lost art. A B.I.B.B.A. Leaflet. E. Nobbs, 1969.

A Manual of Beekeeping. J. Hunter, 1876.

The Nature Ordering and Preserving of Bees. G. Markham, 1614.

Old West Surrey. G. Jekyll, 1978.

One Thousand Years of Devon Beekeeping. R. H. Brown, 1975.

The Practical Beemaster. J. Keys, 1780.

Skeps. British Beekeepers' Association Leaflet No. 1. Undated but late 19th Century.

Straw and Straw Craftsmen. A. Staniforth, 1981.

List of Photographs

Index

103

www.ingramcontent.com/pod-product-compliance
Lightning Source LLC
Chambersburg PA
CBHW052048270326
41931CB00012B/2682